# ARSENAL
## A PICTORIAL HISTORY

# ARSENAL
## A PICTORIAL HISTORY

**COMPILED BY**
**NEAL SIMPSON   KEVIN ALCOCK**

BREEDON
BOOKS
SPORT

First published in Great Britain by
The Breedon Books Publishing Company Limited
44 Friar Gate, Derby DE1 1DA
1992.

ISBN 1 873626 26 6

Printed and bound by The Bath Press Limited, Bath and London.
Jacket printed by BDC Printing Services Ltd of Derby.

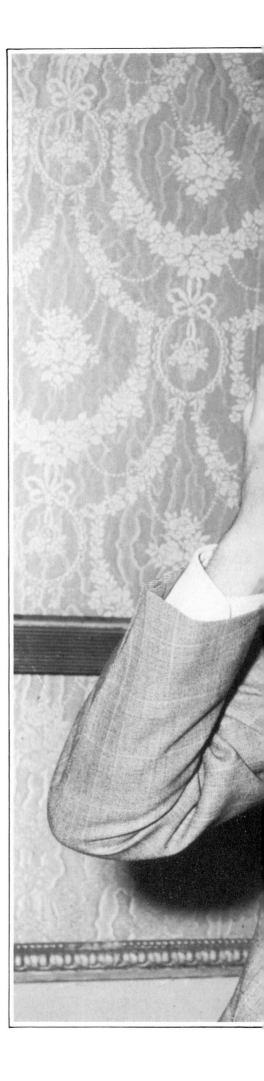

# Introduction

THIS book is the first in a series of Pictorial History titles which, it is planned, will eventually cover all the major clubs in the Football League. It is particularly significant that the series should begin with Arsenal, still arguably the greatest club name in the world.

The book uses photographs from a number of sources, but mainly the Hulton-Deutsch Collection and the Empics Agency of Nottingham, whose files include not only work taken by their own photographers but also those of Peter Robinson, the official FIFA photographer.

The result is a work which tells, in vivid photographic detail, the story of Arsenal from the last century, through their magnificent era of the 1930s, through the post-war years and every decade since. Indeed, there is hardly a season after World War One which is not represented here.

It is hoped that these images, from the days of short back and sides and baggy shorts to the time of 'Beatle' haircuts and the new 'Continental' strips and right up to the game's modern look, will bring back memories of the games and players to those supporters lucky enough to remember them, and also fire the imagination of younger fans who can now see just how their club's famous story developed.

# ARSENAL
## Football Club

---
*Honours*
---

### Football League Champions

1930-31, 1932-33, 1933-34, 1934-35, 1937-38,
1947-48, 1952-53, 1970-71, 1988-89, 1990-91

### Runners-up

1925-26, 1931-32, 1972-73

### Second Division Runners-up

1903-04

### FA Cup Winners

1929-30, 1935-36, 1949-50, 1970-71, 1978-79

### Runners-up

1926-27, 1931-32, 1951-52, 1971-72, 1977-78, 1979-80

### Football League Cup Winners

1986-87

### Runners-up

1967-68, 1968-69, 1987-88

### European Fairs Cup Winners

1969-70

### European Cup-winners' Cup Runners-up

1979-80

The Royal Arsenal Football Club pictured
in 1888-9, two years after the club was
formed as Dial Square FC. In this season,
the club played a full programme of
friendly games against such teams as
Tottenham Hotspur, London Caledonians
and Millwall Rovers. They also competed
in the London Association Cup, when they
were knocked out by Clapton in the semi-
final, and in the Kent Cup, when they were
disqualified for refusing to play extra-time
after a 3-3 draw with Gravesend. Alas, the
names of the players on this earliest known
team group of the club have long been lost.

Half-back William Julian joined Royal Arsenal in the summer of 1889 from Boston Town. Julian skippered the club and when he left for Luton Town in the summer of 1892, he had made over 100 senior appearances for the Gunners.

Woolwich Arsenal in 1900-01, the season in which the club finished seventh in Division Two and went out of the FA Cup to West Brom in the second round. Back row (left to right): Dr Clark (chairman), F.Warman (assistant trainer), Fred Coles, Duncan McNichol, Andy Main, Tom Spicer, Jimmy Jackson, Walter Place, J.Hindle (trainer), Harry Bradshaw (manager). Middle: Tom Low, John Dick, John Blackwood, Peter Turner, James Tennant. Front: Alex McCowie, John Anderson, Tom Grieve.

Woolwich Arsenal defenders appeal for offside against Manchester United at Clayton in March 1906. The Gunners won this FA Cup quarter-final tie 3-2 but lost to Newcastle United in the semi-final at Stoke.

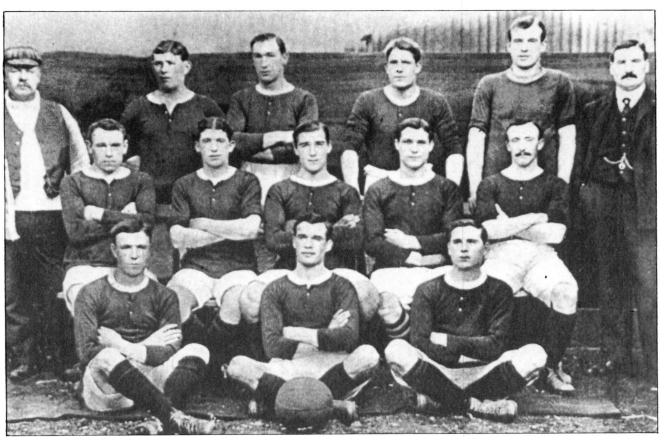

The Woolwich Arsenal party which visited Europe in May 1906, playing games in Berlin, Prague, Budapest and Vienna. Back row (left to right): Dunmore (trainer), Jimmy Sharp, James Ashcroft, Percy Sands, Archie Cross, Phil Kelso (manager). Middle: Archie Gray, Bobby Templeton, Andy Ducat, Tom Fitchie, Roddy McEachrane; Front: James Bellamy, John Dick, James Blair.

Woolwich Arsenal's Peter Kyle heads for goal in the goalless FA Cup first-round game against Hull City at Plumstead in January 1908. Kyle scored in the replay but Hull won 4-1.

Woolwich Arsenal playing staff at the beginning of the 1911-12 season. Back row (left to right): J.Peart, G.Grant, J.Shaw, G.Burdett, H.Crawford, A.Gray, D.Neave. Middle: Mr A.Keard (honorary secretary), G.Hardy (trainer), A.Calvert, F.Gatenby, A.Ducat, M.Thomson, P.Sands, A.Common, C.Lewis, W.Rippon, J.W.Humble (director), J.Dick (coach and assistant trainer). Front: J.Flanagan, A.McKinnon, L.Calder, J.Chalmers, G.Morrell (manager-secretary), T.Winship, P.Greenaway, L.Rippon, R.McEachrane. The Gunners finished tenth in Division One and went out of the FA Cup in the first round.

Woolwich Arsenal playing staff at the beginning of the 1911-12 season. Back row (left to right): J.Peart, G.Grant, J.Shaw, G.Burdett, H.Crawford, A.Gray, D.Neave. Middle: Mr A.Keard (honorary secretary), G.Hardy (trainer), A.Calvert, F.Gatenby, A.Ducat, M.Thomson, P.Sands, A.Common, C.Lewis, W.Rippon, J.W.Humble (director), J.Dick (coach and assistant trainer). Front: J.Flanagan, A.McKinnon, L.Calder, G.Morrell (manager-secretary), T.Winship, P.Greenaway, L.Rippon, R.McEachrane. The Gunners finished tenth in Division One and went out of the FA Cup in the first round.

In April 1912, Woolwich Arsenal met Tottenham Hotspur at the White City Stadium in this match in aid of the Titanic Disaster Fund. Arsenal won 3-0 with goals from Hanks, Greenaway and Thomson before a crowd of only 5,000, almost all of whom were apparently out of the camera's view!

Manchester United goalkeeper Bob Beale comes under pressure at the Manor Ground, Plumstead, on the opening day of the 1912-13 season. United, League Champions in 1911, were held to a goalless draw by the Gunners, who ended the season relegated to the Second Division.

Bolton Wanderers under attack at Plumstead in September 1912. A crowd of 13,000 saw Arsenal lose 2-1.

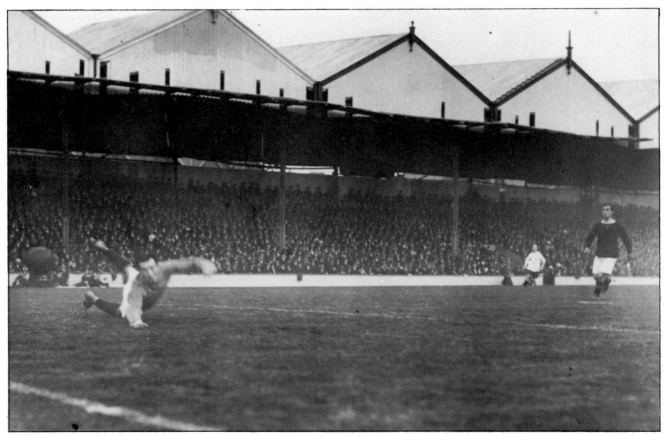

Arsenal goalkeeper John Caldwell saves this shot from a Bury forward at the Gunners' new home at Highbury in October 1913, but the Lancashire side won 1-0, although the Gunners eventually finished third in Division Two. This was the last of Caldwell's three League games for Arsenal. He was standing in for the injured Joe Lievesley and the following summer was transferred to Reading for a second spell with the Berkshire club.

In October 1913, Arsenal signed England winger Jock Rutherford from Newcastle United. This picture shows Rutherford with some of his new colleagues. From left to right: George Hardy (trainer), Joe Lievesley, Steve Stonley, John Flanagan, George Jobey, Rutherford and Joe Shaw. Rutherford was to have three separate spells with the Gunners and altogether scored 25 goals in 222 League appearances for the club.

On 30 August 1919, the Football League resumed after World War One and Arsenal, despite finishing the last pre-war season fifth in Division Two, found themselves in Division One after some behind-the-scenes wheeling and dealing by their chairman Sir Henry Norris. Here, skipper Joe Shaw meets his Newcastle United counterpart Billy McCracken before the first match of the new era. Newcastle won 1-0 in front of a 40,000 crowd at Highbury.

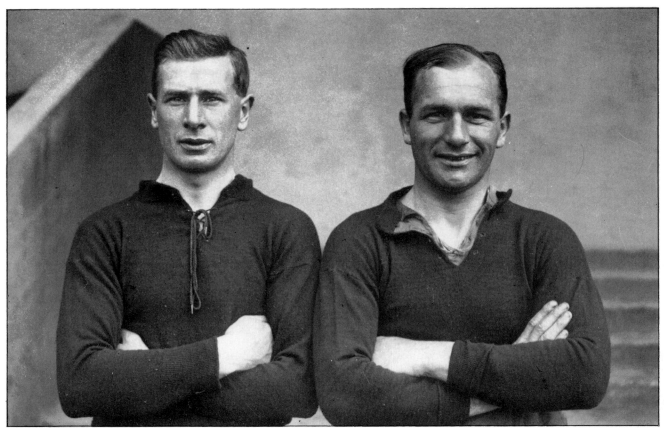

Arsenal players Bobby Turnbull (left) and Andrew Kennedy before the start of the 1922-3 season. Turnbull, who joined the Gunners from Army football, was converted from left-back to centre-forward in an emergency and finished the season as top scorer with 20 goals. Altogether he scored 26 goals in 59 League games before being transferred to Charlton Athletic in November 1924. Kennedy, also a left-back, had just signed from Crystal Palace and went on to make 122 League appearances for Arsenal before moving to Everton in January 1928.

Centre-forward Harry Woods scores Arsenal's second goal against Luton Town in the first round of the FA Cup in January 1924, but in the next round the Gunners were knocked out by Cardiff City. A crowd of 37,500 watched the game against the Hatters at Highbury. Woods was later transferred to Luton.

The 1924-5 season was a black one for the Gunners, who ended it in 20th place and just missed relegation. In February, Huddersfield Town came to Highbury and won 5-0. This picture shows one of Arsenal's rare raids as Huddersfield goalkeeper Billy Mercer punches the ball over the bar with Jimmy Brain in attendance.

For 1925-6 the offside law was changed and the result was a hatful of goals. On the opening day of the season, however, there were no goals for Arsenal, who lost 1-0 at home to Spurs. Here Cock (right) stretches for the ball as Arthur Grimsdell moves in.

Tottenham goalkeeper Hinton grabs the ball as Jack Cock challenges. A crowd of more than 53,000 saw the game on Saturday, 29 August 1925.

The 1925-6 season saw the Gunners finish runners-up to Huddersfield in Herbert Chapman's first season in charge at Highbury. Here, Arsenal are attacking the Bolton goal during their 3-2 home defeat by the Trotters in October. Players (from left to right) are: Jimmy Seddon (Bolton), Charlie Buchan (Arsenal), Harry Greenhalgh (Bolton), Dick Pymm (Bolton's goalkeeper), Jimmy Brain (Arsenal) and Bob Haworth (Bolton). The attendance was over 41,000.

Arsenal's debutant goalkeeper Scottish international Bill Harper dives to cut out a low centre during the 6-1 win over Bury at Highbury in November 1925. Harper, who joined Arsenal from Hibs for the big fee of £4,000, made 63 League appearances before leaving at the end of the following season to play for Fall River FC in the USA.

Jimmy Brain heads one of his two goals in Arsenal's 3-2 win over newly-promoted Manchester United at a snowbound Highbury in January 1926. The United goalkeeper is Alf Steward.

Against Manchester United in January 1926, Jock Rutherford, by now coming towards the end of his Arsenal career, shows that he has lost none of his trickery. Rutherford first joined the Gunners in October 1913, then left to manage Stoke towards the end of 1922-3 but returned to Highbury as a player in August 1923. He retired in the 1925 close season but was re-signed to play in a handful of games after Christmas. He went to Clapton Orient in August 1926 before retiring altogether in the summer of 1927

Charlie Buchan leads out Arsenal. Buchan had played for the Gunners as an amateur in 1909-10 but fell out with them over the payment of expenses and eventually signed for Sunderland after a spell with Gravesend & Northfleet and Leyton. It then cost Arsenal a fee of £2,000 plus £100 for every goal he scored in his first season, when he rejoined the club in 1925, at the age of 35. His 20 League and Cup goals in that first campaign doubled the fee, but he led them to a League Championship runners-up spot and later to an FA Cup Final.

A crowd of 38,842 saw this 2-2 draw against Newcastle United at Highbury in October 1926. Newcastle's Stan Seymour is robbed of the ball by Tom Parker whilst Charlie Buchan is back in defence.

Jimmy Brain (second left) wheels away after scoring Arsenal's second goal in their 4-2 defeat at Highbury in December 1926. The other Arsenal player is Charlie Buchan.

Buchan (second left) in action again as the Wolves defence looks at sixes and sevens. A crowd of nearly 53,000 watched this sixth round FA Cup tie at Highbury in March 1927.

Brain follows up Arsenal's first goal in the 1927 FA Cup semi-final against Southampton at Stamford Bridge. Some sources credited Joe Hulme with the goal, others gave the Saints' full-back Hough the unwanted distinction of netting an own-goal. Buchan increased the Gunners' lead before Rawlings pulled a goal back for Southampton with five minutes remaining. The other Arsenal players in this picture are Blythe and Hoar.

Wolves goalkeeper Frank George fumbles the ball as Charlie Buchan races in. Arsenal

on this FA Cup quarter-final match 2-1 in March 1927 with goals from Blyth and Butler.

Arsenal pictured before the 1927 FA Cup Final against Cardiff City at Wembley. Back row (left to right): Horace Cope, Alf Baker, Tom Parker, Dan Lewis, Jack Butler, Bob John, Andy Kennedy, Billy Seddon. Front: Tom Whittaker (trainer), Joe Hulme, Charlie Buchan, Jimmy Brain, Billy Blyth, Sid Hoar, Herbert Chapman (manager).

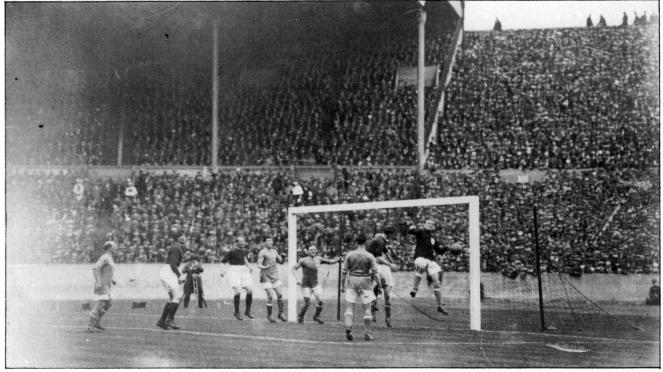

Cardiff's Irish international goalkeeper Tom Farquharson seems to be in some difficulty as Arsenal's Jimmy Brain gets in a header during the 1927 FA Cup Final at Wembley, but somehow the ball was kept out.

Farquharson guards his line as Cardiff get the ball clear. Arsenal's Charlie Buchan (partly hidden) is the danger man but is the subject of close attention from the Bluebirds' defence.

Dan Lewis punches clear from a Cardiff forward at Wembley.

Lewis somehow allows the ball to slip under his body and the FA Cup is on its way out of England for the only time in the history of the competition. Cardiff's centre-forward Hughie Ferguson had tried a long, low shot 15 minutes from time and the ball spun out of the goalkeeper's arms.

The ball is over the line and Cardiff can begin their celebrations.

Sid Hoar, a £3,000 signing from Luton Town in November 1924, clears the ball from danger as two West Brom players move in. Played at Highbury during the third-round FA Cup tie in January 1928, the Gunners won 2-0. Hoar, a former straw-hat maker, was gassed during World War One but recovered to enjoy a good career in the Football League.

Arsenal's Billy Blyth turns away as Jimmy Brain (not in picture) puts the Gunners ahead from Joe Hulme's cross in the fourth-round Cup game against Everton at Highbury in January 1928.

The fifth round of the 1927-8 FA Cup saw an attendance of 58,505 squeeze into Highbury for the game against Aston Villa. Here, police officers bring small boys to the front of the massive crowd.

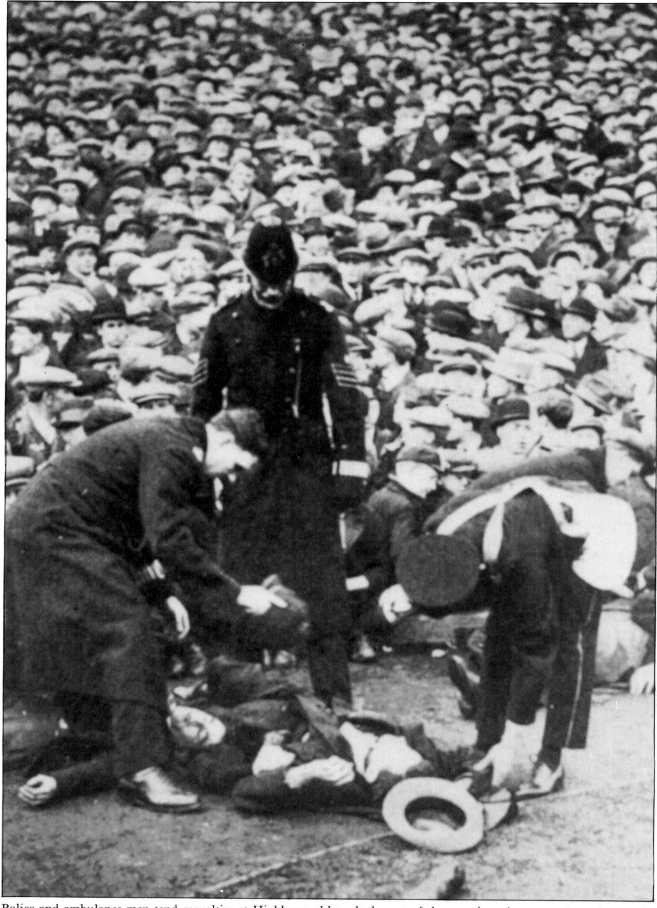

Police and ambulance men tend casualties at Highbury, although the rest of the crowd are intent on the action on the pitch where the Gunners beat Villa 4-1 with goals from Brain (2), Lambert and Hulme. The victory gave Arsenal a quarter-final game against Stoke City, also at home.

The Gunners' FA Cup sixth-round game in March 1928 saw the band of the 2nd North Staffordshire Regiment parade before the kick-off of the game against Stoke City.

Arsenal supporters rival the North Staffordshire band for the crowd's favours.

Stoke goalkeeper Dixon gets a hand to the ball but cannot prevent Brain (centre) from putting Arsenal ahead. Sid Hoar is ready to make certain should the need arise.

This time the action is around the Stoke goal as the Gunners' forwards watch the ball run to safety. Arsenal went on to win 4-1 with two goals each goals from Blyth and Hoar.

Jimmy Brain is again on the hunt for goal but this time he cannot keep the ball in play. Charlie Buchan (far right) stands helpless as the ball runs over the goal-line.

Blackburn Rovers goalkeeper Jock Crawford makes a spectacular leap to tip over an Arsenal shot in the 1928 FA Cup semi-final at Filbert Street. Brain is again lurking in the danger area, but he could not help Arsenal this time and it was the Lancashire side who went to Wembley after beating the Gunners 1-0.

Charlie Buchan (far left) is beaten to the ball by goalkeeper Crawford, who punches it away. Blackburn went on to beat Huddersfield Town in the 1928 Cup Final.

Mansfield Town goalkeeper Staples punches clear at Highbury in February 1929. Mansfield, who were then in the Midland League, had fought through to the fourth round of the FA Cup from the qualifying competition, but their dream ended when Arsenal beat them 2-0 in front of 44,000 fans.

Swindon Town goalkeeper Nash attempts to block a shot from Arsenal centre-forward David Jack in the FA Cup fifth-round replay at Highbury in February 1929. The Gunners followed up earlier victories over Stoke and Mansfield with a 2-1 win over the Wiltshire club — after the sides had drawn 0-0 at the County Ground — but went out 1-0 to Aston Villa in the quarter-final.

Combining business with pleasure. Manager Herbert Chapman was a keen golfer and once a week he took his Arsenal players for a round at Hatch End, Middlesex. From left to right are Tom Parker, Alex James, David Jack and Chapman, pictured in November 1929.

Bob John and Tom Parker combine to beat a Burnley forward at Highbury in September 1929. Goalkeeper Charlie Preedy waits for the back pass. Burnley were on their way out of the First Division and Arsenal, who were to finish only 14th themselves, beat the Clarets 6-1.

The crowds are already pouring into Highbury, although there is still well over an hour to the kick-off between Arsenal and Chelsea in the third round of the FA Cup in January 1930. The biggest crowd of the day — 55,579 — saw Arsenal win 2-0 with goals from Lambert and Bastin.

Arsenal (in white shirts) attacking the West Ham goal in the sixth-round tie at Upton Park in March 1930. The Gunners won 3-0, Lambert (2) and Baker scoring.

At Elland Road, Leeds, in March 1930, Arsenal looked to be out of the FA Cup. With more than an hour gone of the semi-final against bottom of the Second Division Hull City, the Gunners trailed 2-0. Then David Jack pulled back a goal from Hulme's centre and eight minutes from the end, with Hull having only nine fit men, Cliff Bastin curled a shot into the Tigers' net to force a replay. In this picture, Arsenal goalkeeper Dan Lewis watches the ball flash past his right-hand post as Hull mount an attack early in the game.

David Jack hammers home the goal which beat Hull City in the 1930 FA Cup semi-final replay at Villa Park. This was one of the most important goals in the history of the club, ultimately leading to their first FA Cup Final victory, which turned out to be the beginning of Arsenal's greatest era.

The Tigers' goalkeeper Fred Gibson is beaten and Jack begins to turn away, although in those more restrained days a brief handshake was the most he could expect from delighted colleagues. The hugging and kissing so common today would have been anathema to the sportsman of the pre-war era. Earlier in the game, Hull's Arthur Childs had been sent off for aiming a kick at Alex James.

Tom Parker (Arsenal) and Tommy Wilson (Huddersfield Town) lead out their respective sides for the 1930 FA Cup Final at Wembley.

A cinema newsreel camera records the Arsenal party during a break in training before the 1930 FA Cup Final. Manager the distance, by the fence, is trainer Tom Whittaker (hatless).

Herbert Chapman is flanked by Joe Hulme and Charlie Preedy. Skipper Tom Parker is standing behind Chapman. In

Parker and Wilson shake hands before the toss-up. The referee is Mr T.Crewe of Leicester.

The sinister shape of the German Graf Zeppelin flies over Wembley Stadium to temporarily distract the 92,486 crowd at the 1930 FA Cup Final.

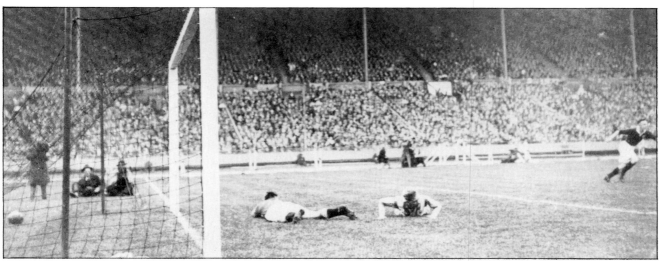

The 1930 Cup Final is just over a quarter of an hour old and Arsenal take the lead through James, who scored with a low drive after Cliff Bastin delivered the final pass.

Arsenal goalkeeper Charlie Preedy grabs the ball from marauding Huddersfield forwards.

Jack Lambert (extreme left) takes a pass from James and gets in a shot between two Huddersfield defenders and the goalkeeper to put Arsenal 2-0 ahead.

Parker leads Arsenal off the field at the end of the 1930 Cup Final.

In August 1930, Arsenal signed Gerard Keyser, a Dutch-born goalkeeper, who had been playing for Margate. Originally, the Home Office allowed Keyser to remain in Britain and play for Arsenal, only if he was not paid by the club, instead representing his father's fruit import business in Covent Garden. Eventually he was allowed to sign professional forms, in May 1931. He made only 12 League appearances but did play in the 1930 FA Charity Shield game before being transferred to Charlton. Here, Keyser collects the ball as two Leeds United forwards rush in during the League game at Highbury in September 1930.

Arsenal fans with the famous duck mascot before the start of the FA Cup third-round tie against Aston Villa in January 1931. The sides drew 2-2 at Highbury before Hulme (2) and Jack put the Gunners through at Villa Park.

In 1930-31, Arsenal became the first southern club to win the League Championship, and they also lifted the FA Charity Shield as well as a host of minor trophies. Their defence of the FA Cup, however, was not successful and Chelsea knocked them out in the fourth round at Stamford Bridge. This photograph shows Chelsea's second goal, scored by George Mills from a centre by Alex Jackson. The Arsenal goalkeeper is Bill Harper, who had just returned from American soccer.

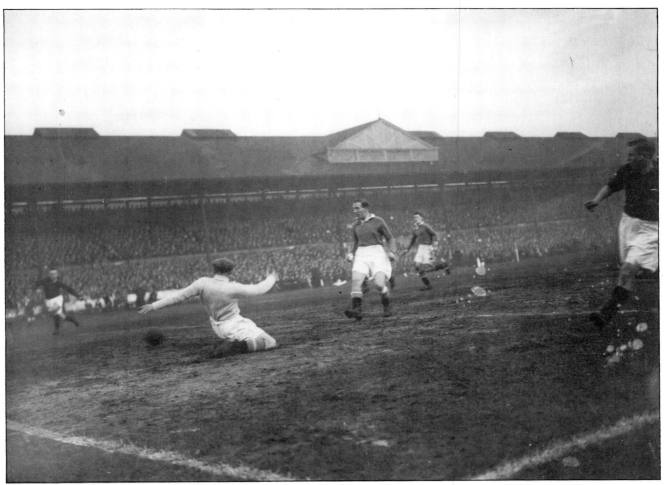

Cliff Bastin (extreme right) scores Arsenal's goal in the Cup defeat at Stamford Bridge in 1931.

Arsenal players and officials pictured in April 1931 with their trophies including the

League Championship (third from left) and the FA Charity Shield (second from right).

Arsenal pictured in 1931-2, the season they finished runners-up to Everton and lost to Newcastle United in the FA Cup Final. Back row (left to right): Tom Parker, Charlie Jones, Frank Moss, Herbie Roberts, Bob John, Tom Black. Front row: Herbert Chapman (manager), Joe Hulme, David Jack, Jack Lambert, Alex James, Cliff Bastin, Tom Whittaker (trainer). Black did not appear in a League game for Arsenal and the following season, within a week of the Gunners' humiliating Cup defeat by Walsall, he was transferred to Plymouth Argyle.

Charlie Preedy gathers the ball from Aston Villa forward Billy Walker at Highbury in October 1931 while Tom Parker covers the Arsenal 'keeper. The game ended in a 1-1 draw before 54,951 spectators.

Joe Hulme is in the back of the net after scoring Arsenal's first goal against non-League Darwen at Highbury in January 1932 in the third round of the FA Cup. Arsenal won 11-1 with Bastin scoring four goals.

Bastin falls over the Darwen goalkeeper as he scores Arsenal's eighth goal.

Another crush at Highbury. An injured
fan is passed over spectators' heads
during the fourth-round Cup game
against Plymouth in January 1932, when
a crowd of 65,386 saw Arsenal win 4-2.

Alex James missed this penalty against Blackpool in February 1932 but the Gunners still won the First Division game
2-0 with goals from Jack and Parkin.

Joe Hulme's goal gave Arsenal a 1-0 home win over Newcastle United in a League match in March 1932. A few weeks later the sides met in the Cup Final at Wembley. In this picture, Herbie Roberts challenges the Magpies' Jack Allen at Highbury.

From left to right: Bob John, Herbert Chapman and Alex James chatting before the 1932 FA Cup Final.

Arsenal and Newcastle United take to the field at Wembley for the 1932 FA Cup Final.

King George V is introduced to the Arsenal team by Tom Parker.

Arsenal centre-forward David Jack climbs high but Newcastle goalkeeper Albert McInroy has little trouble in collecting the ball.

This time Jack gets his head to the ball but again Newcastle got the danger away.

Arsenal goalkeeper Frank Moss clutches at the ball as Jack Allen rushes in. Arsenal centre-half Herbie Roberts is the defender.

Joe Hulme scores the Gunners' first goal against Sunderland at Highbury in September 1932. Hulme went on to net a hat-trick as the Wearsiders were hammered 6-1. It was Arsenal's third game of the season — they had won at Birmingham and lost at home to West Brom — and by the end of the campaign they were crowned League Champions, the first of a hat-trick of titles.

'Tim' Coleman scores one of his two goals against Middlesbrough at Highbury in November 1932.

During their 1932-3 Championship season, Arsenal scored some big wins. In October they scored eight goals without reply past Leicester City. Above and below shows an effort by Joe Hulme, which would have given the Gunners an even earlier lead, but was ruled out for offside.

Leicester goalkeeper Calvert nips out to snatch the ball off the feet of David Jack, who was restricted to one goal as the Gunners went on the rampage.

Herbert Chapman was a great innovator and one of his suggestions was that football could be played under floodlights. In November 1932, a conference to discuss floodlit soccer was held at the Great Eastern Hotel, Liverpool Street. The previous evening representatives of several clubs attended this demonstration of 'experimental football by floodlight' at Highbury.

Arsenal could not have had too many sleepless nights when they drew Third Division South club Walsall in the 1932-3 FA Cup, even though the tie was to be played at the Midlanders' ground. But what followed was one of the biggest Cup shocks of all time as Walsall triumphed 2-0. Here, three days before one of the blackest days in Arsenal's history, Alex James, Frank Hill (a £3,000 signing from Aberdeen), Herbie Roberts and Cliff Bastin practise heading on a raw morning at Highbury.

In December 1933, the famous amateur side Corinthians organised instructional classes for young boys at Highbury. This photograph shows the Corinthians' G.N.Foster with Arsenal's Herbert Chapman. The Arsenal boss was now a legendary name in football, a great innovator who had set Huddersfield Town on the road to the first-ever hat-trick of League Championships before taking over at Highbury in 1925 and who had now put the Gunners on a similar road. Alas, Chapman was not to see the crowning glory of Arsenal's triple success, for in January 1934 he died suddenly.

Arsenal were also one of the pioneers of playing against foreign opposition and in December 1933 they met a Vienna XI at Highbury and won 4-2 with goals from Bastin (2), Hulme and Jack. One of Bastin's goals was this penalty which the Viennese goalkeeper Platzer seems to have made a hash of stopping.

This goal, laid on by Bastin and finished off by Jimmy Dunne, saved Arsenal some red faces at Luton in January 1934, when the Gunners played badly but managed to scrape into the fourth round of the FA Cup 1-0. Dunne, an Irish international, joined Arsenal from Sheffield United for £8,250 but made only 32 League and Cup appearances before being transferred to Southampton for £2,000.

In the fifth round of the FA Cup in February 1934, Champions Arsenal beat Derby County, then top of the First Division, 1-0 with a goal from David Jack, in front of nearly 67,000 fans at Highbury. Here, Jack is on floor and the Derby defence manage to scramble the ball away.

Alex James challenges Derby goalkeeper Jack Kirby.

This time Jack's outstretched boot cannot reach the ball and Derby's defence can breathe again.

An example of the camaraderie which existed at Highbury in the 1930s. Manager George Allison sets himself up for the cameraman as a stand-in goalkeeper. The purpose of the session was to feature the Gunners' new signing, George Holden, a 17-year-old from Darwen in Lancashire. Alas, Holden did not make the grade at Highbury.

In 1935-6, Arsenal's remarkable run of League Championship successes came to an end and the Gunners finished sixth in Division One as Sunderland took the title. But Arsenal were still a team to be feared and in October 1935, Blackburn came to Highbury and were hammered 5-1. Here, Ted Drake and Alex James put the Lancashire defence under pressure.

Cliff Bastin gets in his shot and appears to have knocked a Birmingham defender off his feet in the process. Arsenal drew 1-1 with the Blues in January 1936.

Ted Drake scores the only goal of the match against Stoke City at Highbury in February 1936. The Potters' goalkeeper Wilkinson has no chance at point-blank range.

In 1936, Wimbledon tennis star Fred Perry accepted an offer to train at Highbury under the watchful eye of Tom Whittaker. Players crouching (left to right) are Denis Compton, Herbie Roberts, Cliff Bastin, Perry, George Male and Joe Hulme.

George Barber of Chelsea gets the better of a heading duel with Ted Drake at Highbury in April 1936. Drake scored in the 1-1 draw. Work has begun on the East Stand on Avenell Road. It cost £130,000 and was opened six months later to accommodate over 8,000 spectators.

The 1936 FA Cup Final between Arsenal and Sheffield United. The Blades' goalkeeper Smith makes a desperate grab f

e ball right on his own goal-line as Ray Bowden attempts to elbow him over the line. Drake is the other Arsenal player.

This time Smith can only look in dismay as Drake's shot finds the back of the net for the only goal of the 1936 Cup Final.

Arsenal, wearing unfamiliar hooped shirts because of a clash of colours, on the attack against Barnsley in an FA Cup quarter-final tie at Highbury in February 1936. The Gunners had knocked out Bristol Rovers, Liverpool and Newcastle United (after a replay).

The 1936-7 season saw Arsenal without a major trophy for the first time in some years. On the opening day of the season they beat Everton 3-2. Here goalkeeper Alex Wilson and centre-half Roberts combine to keep out Everton's prolific centre-forward Dixie Dean. Wilson later became physiotherapist to Kent CCC and in 1967 went to the United States to work with Boston Beacons in the American Soccer League.

In September 1936, the Gunners beat the League Champions, Sunderland, 4-1 at Highbury, where nearly 57,000 fans saw this clash of the First Division giants. Here, Eddie Hapgood launches himself into a flying tackle against Duns, the Wearsiders' outside-right.

Arsenal's FA Cup campaign of 1936-7 saw some high scores before they were eliminated by West Brom in the quarter-finals. The Gunners beat Chesterfield 5-1, Manchester United 5-0 and Burnley 7-1 on their way to the last eight. On the eve of the fifth-round game against Burnley, Alex James, sporting a natty piece of headgear, and a young Denis Compton lap the Highbury pitch.

Arsenal's 1936-7 season ended on a mediocre note with a defeat at Stamford Bridge and a home draw with Bolton Wanderers. In this picture, the Pensioners launch another attack on the visitors' goal. The 'keeper is Frank Boulton.

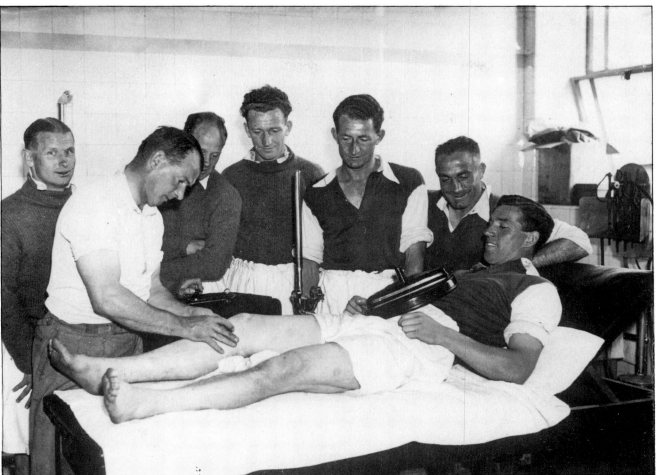

Arsenal's Alf Kirchen was injured against Everton on the opening day of the 1937-8 season and on the following Monday, he was on the treatment table under the supervision of Tom Whittaker. Other Arsenal players called in to watch, obviously for the benefit of the cameraman, are (from left to right) Cliff Bastin, George Male, Herbert Roberts, Jack Crayston and Wilf Copping.

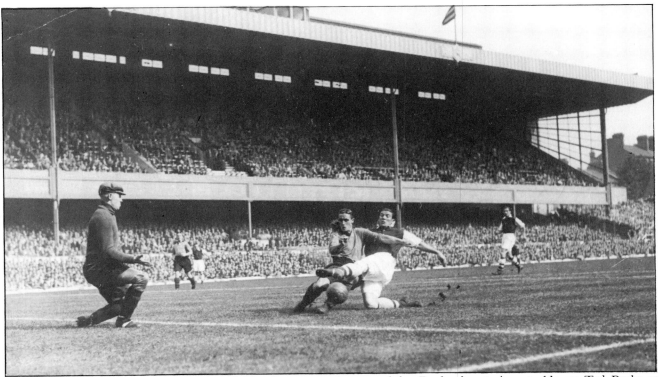

Wolverhampton Wanderers right-back Bill Morris, soon to be capped for England, gets in a tackle on Ted Drake at Highbury in September 1937. The Wolves goalkeeper is Alex Scott. Drake scored twice in Arsenal's 5-0 win and Arsenal were on their way to another League Championship.

Manchester City goalkeeper Frank Swift gets his fingers to the ball as Arsenal's new signing George Hunt topples over. Hunt, just signed from Spurs, was making his debut for the Gunners in this 2-1 win watched by 68,353 spectators at Highbury in October 1937.

George Swindin tips the ball away from a crowd of players including Grimsby Town's Hughie Gallacher at Highbury in March 1938. Despite the presence of the former Scotland star, the Mariners went down 5-1.

This time Swindin dives to save a Charlton penalty in April 1938. The result was a 2-2 draw which helped the Gunners towards yet another Championship success.

Moods can change dramatically at an important football match and for managers that is especially true. This sequence of photographs shows the changing face of Arsenal boss George Allison as he watches his team defeat Stoke City 4-1 at Highbury in December 1938.

Brentford's Crozier dives bravely at the feet of Ted Drake at Griffin Park in September 1938. The Bees won this First Division game 1-0.

Arsenal's visit to Stamford Bridge in October 1938 saw the Gunners go down 4-2. George Swindin looks in trouble here, diving at the feet of Chelsea's Adolf Hanson. Eddie Hapgood is about to hook the ball to safety. A year later, poor Hanson was burdened with one of the most unpopular first names in history!

In August 1938, a 16-year-old lad is cutting the grass at Highbury and dreaming about a career in League football. He can hardly be with a more famous club, yet war was just around the corner and destiny decreed that when his career finally got under way, young Len Shackleton's fame would be found, not on the hallowed turf of Highbury but first back in his native Bradford and then with Sunderland.

In February 1939, with war clouds looming over Europe, Arsenal manager George Allison addresses a Highbury crowd of 54,510 about the need for 'moral rearmament in sport'. After Allison and other sporting personalities — racing driver Captain G.E.T.Eyston, British heavyweight boxing champion Len Harvey and tennis star H.W.Austin, had spoken, the match against Chelsea got under way and the Gunners won 1-0.

In July 1939, Highbury was transformed into a film set for the shooting of *The Arsenal Stadium Mystery*. The players were contracted for two weeks to take part in the story of a dressing-room murder. In this picture the Gunners players take a break alongside the professional cast who were members of an imaginary club called 'The Argonauts FC'.

Chelsea's Vic Woodley punches the ball away from Ted Drake of Arsenal as the away side's left-back Jack Smith watches. Arsenal's Gordon Bremner scored the only goal of the game at Highbury in February 1939.

Former Everton and England star Joe Mercer was signed by the Gunners in 1946 and revitalised his own career at Highbury.

Manchester United goalkeeper Bill Fielding is well beaten and full-back John Aston, too, cannot prevent Ronnie Rooke's goal at a snow-covered Highbury in February 1947. It was one of Rooke's hat-trick as United were hammered 6-2.

Arsenal's first-team squad pictured at the start of the 1947-8 season. Back row (left to right): George Male, Archie Macaulay, Paddy Sloan, Alf Fields. Middle: Billy Milne (trainer), Bryn Jones, Laurie Scott, George Swindin, Walley Barnes, Joe Mercer, Tom Whittaker (manager). Front: Don Roper, Jimmy Logie, Reg Lewis, Ronnie Rooke, Ian McPherson. Former player Billy Milne, who won the DCM in France during World War One, had just taken over as first-team trainer.

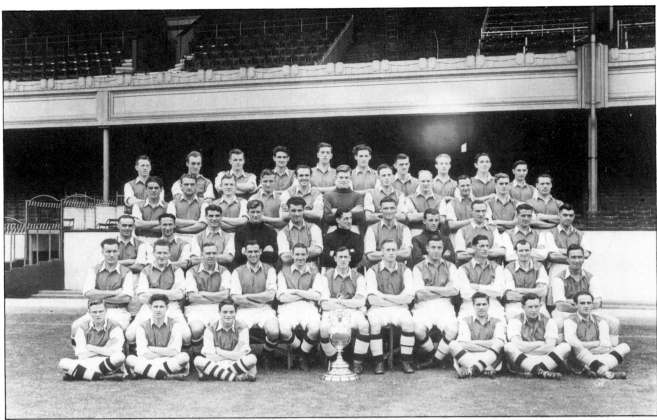

The Arsenal playing staff pictured with the Football League Championship trophy in 1948, after the Gunners finished seven points ahead of Manchester United. Manager Tom Whittaker had made some inspired signings including those of veterans Joe Mercer and Ronnie Rooke. Mercer (seated immediately behind the trophy) led the Gunners to their sixth League title. Rooke (third from the right, seated) scored 33 League goals.

As the Gunners powered their way to the First Division championship in 1947-8, three former stars, whose careers began in the days of Royal Arsenal, watch from the side-lines. From left to right are Bill Julian (wing-half, 1889-92), Gavin Crawford (winger or half-back, 1891-98) and John McBean (left-back, 1888-92).

Veteran Ronnie Rooke, who along with Joe Mercer provided the experience as Arsenal lifted the title again.

Arsenal's team which lost 1-0 at Villa Park in January 1949. Back row (left to right): Archie Macaulay, Walley Barnes, George Swindin, Billy Milne (trainer), Lionel Smith, Joe Mercer. Front: Don Roper, Jimmy Logie, Ronnie Rooke, Doug Lishman, Ian McPherson, Leslie Compton.

Denis Compton scores Arsenal's second goal against Burnley in the fifth round of the FA Cup in February 1950. Earlier, Reg Lewis had given the Gunners the lead. A crowd of 55,458 saw the match which earned Arsenal a home quarter-final tie against Leeds United.

Arsenal centre-half Leslie Compton challenges Chelsea goalkeeper Harry Medhurst at Highbury in April 1949. Chelsea won 2-1.

Arsenal full-back Lionel Smith, who made 180 League and Cup appearances between 1948 and 1954.

Arsenal's Alex Forbes cannot block this cross from Reg Kirkham of Burnley.

Arsenal's Leslie Compton hammers the ball away from Liverpool's Albert Stubbins in the 1950 FA Cup Final at Wembley. The Gunners won 2-0, both goals being scored by Reg Lewis.

Liverpool goalkeeper Cyril Sidlow and Arsenal's Peter Goring both appear to have missed the ball. The Liverpool defender is Eddie Spicer.

Back on the Wembley turf, Joe Mercer is chaired by his victorious teammates after the Gunners' defeat of Liverpool.

Arsenal skipper Joe Mercer receives the FA Cup from His Majesty King George VI

Queen Elizabeth looks on. FA secretary Stanley Rous is to the King's right.

Cup winners Arsenal pictured on the steps of Islington Town Hall before a Civic Reception to mark their 1950 Wembley triumph. Joe Mercer lifts the Cup once more.

Arsenal's playing and coaching staff photographed in October 1950 with the FA Cup. Back row (left to right): J.Chenhall, R.Barr, D.Tilley, D.Oakes, C.Holton, R.Marden, T.Vallance. Third row: E.Stanley, D.Rossiter, W.Healey, D.Bowen, L.Davies, G.Dunkley, P.Hancock, C.Grimshaw, L.Wills, J.Gray, H.Dove, F.Grosvenor. Second row: A.James, G.Male, K.Atkinson, R.Daniel, A.Shaw, E.Platt, L.Compton, G.Swindin, A.Forbes, J.Kelsey, A.Fields, J.Wade, J.Holland, E.Collett, D.Cripps. Front row: H.Owen, J.Crayston, I.McPherson, L.Scott, D.Roper, R.Lewis, J.Mercer, T.Whittaker (manager), W.Barnes, L.Swift, P.Goring, D.Lishman, N.Smith, W.Milne, J.E.Shaw. On ground: A.Milton, M.Ryan, J.Logie, F.Cox, R.Poulton, D.Bennett.

George Swindin gets down at the feet of Manchester United's Jack Rowley at Highbury in October 1950. Lionel Smith is also trying to work the ball away from the prolific United goalscorer. Arsenal won 3-0.

Cliff Holton scores Arsenal's second goal against Huddersfield Town on the opening day of the 1951-2 season. The result was a 2-2 draw.

Arsenal's Walley Barnes (number 2) heads away as George Swindin, Lionel Smith, Joe Mercer and Ray Daniel watch anxiously. The Gunners won this First Division game against Burnley, beating the Clarets 1-0 — the goal from Reg Lewis — in October 1951.

Later the same month, Arsenal beat Fulham 4-3. Here, Doug Flack, the Cottagers' goalkeeper, grabs at the ball as Holton tries to get in a header. Fulham centre-half Bill Pavitt also attempts to thwart the Gunners' centre-forward.

Jimmy Logie is on the ball as Burnley left-back Harold Mather thinks about a tackle in October 1951.

Freddie Cox scores Arsenal's second goal against Luton Town at Kenilworth Road in the quarter-final of the FA Cup in March 1952. Bernard Streten is the helpless goalkeeper, Syd Owen the defender nearest the camera. The Gunners won 3-2.

December 1951 and Arsenal manager Tom Whittaker discusses a point with trainer Billy Milne, who played for the Gunners after World War One. Arsenal were still the innovators in the game. Their supporters' club, founded in 1949, boasted 13,000 members and the club had just chartered a Dakota aircraft to take supporters to a match against Racing Club de Paris.

Ray Daniel and Fulham's Bedford Jezzard in a heading duel at Craven Cottage in March 1952, when a crowd of 46,000 packed into the picturesque ground and saw a goalless draw. The Gunners finished the season in third place. Poor Fulham, though, were relegated after ending the campaign bottom of the table.

George Swindin punches clear during the 1952 FA Cup semi-final against Chelsea at White Hart Lane. The Chelsea number 10 is Roy Bentley.

Arsenal met Newcastle United at Wembley and were beaten 1-0. Alex Forbes and the Magpies' Bobby Mitchell in action.

Doug Lishman beats Joe Harvey to get in a header at the Newcastle goal, where Ronnie Simpson, Tommy Walker and Cliff Holton are lining up.

Arsenal pictured in early August 1952. Back row (left to right): Ray Daniel, Don Roper, George Swindin, Walley Barnes, Doug Lishman, Freddie Cox. Front: Alex Forbes, Jimmy Logie, Joe Mercer, Lionel Smith, Cliff Holton.

Peter Goring could not reach this ball during the game against Newcastle United at Highbury in October 1952, but the Gunners still won 3-0 on their way to the title. The Newcastle defender nearest the camera in centre-half Frank Brennan.

Blackpool's Harry Johnston cannot stop this shot from Joe Mercer in the sixth round of the FA Cup at Highbury in February 1953. The Gunners went down 2-1 in front of more than 69,000 spectators. Blackpool, of course, went on to win the Cup for the first time in their history, in the famous 'Matthews Final'. For Arsenal, however, there was ample consolation — the Football League Championship once more.

Blackpool's Jackie Mudie and Arsenal's Ray Daniel and Jack Kelsey all appear to have been eluded by the ball during the 1953 Cup quarter-final.

Arsenal with the FA Cup and the FA Charity Shield in 1953. Back row (left to right): Jack Crayston (assistant manager), Arthur Shaw, Don Oakes, Cliff Holton, Arthur Milton, Jack Kelsey, Bill Dodgin, Peter Goring, Len Wills, Reuben Marden, Joe Shaw (reserve-team manager), Billy Milne (trainer). Front: Joe Wade, Don Roper, Lionel Smith, Alex Forbes, Tom Whittaker (manager), Jimmy Logie, Doug Lishman, Walley Barnes, Dave Bowen.

Doug Lishman shoots from point-blank range as Newcastle United goalkeeper Ronnie Simpson prepares to block the effort at Highbury in November 1953. A crowd of 62,456 saw Arsenal win 2-1.

Arsenal began their defence of the Championship in 1953-4 with a most disappointing run which saw them wait until 3 October for their first home League win, over Preston North End. Ironically, the Gunners had beaten Preston two days earlier, also at Highbury, in one of the regular floodlit friendly games that the club then organised. A crowd of 25,039 saw this night-time friendly. Nearly 62,000 people were at the League game 48 hours later.

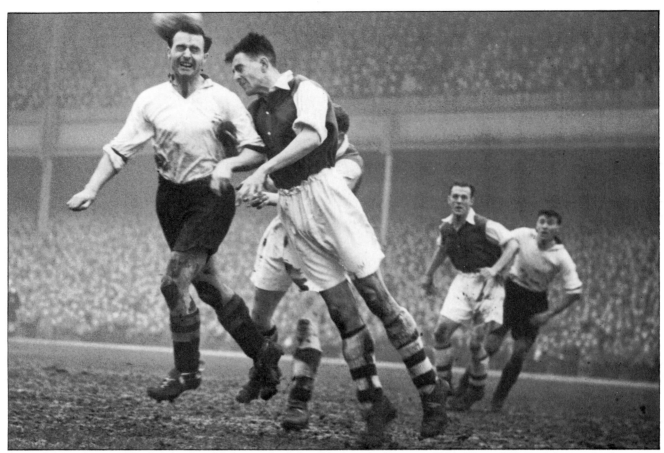

Arsenal beat Aston Villa 5-1 in the third round of the FA Cup in January 1954. Here, Bill Dodgin heads clear from Villa's Dave Walsh. In the next round, however, Third Division South club Norwich City sprang a Cup shock by winning 2-1 at Highbury.

Arsenal lost their first three games of 1954-5, a season in which they nevertheless climbed from 12th the previous campaign to ninth. On Wednesday, 25 August they met newly-promoted Everton at Goodison Park, where over 69,000 spectators saw the Merseysiders win 1-0 with this goal by Tommy Eglington, who headed past Jack Kelsey.

A scramble in front of the Spurs goal at Highbury in September 1954, as Tommy Lawton is beaten by Tottenham goalkeeper Ted Ditchburn. Nearly 54,000 fans saw the Gunners win 2-0, Logie and Lishman scoring. Arsenal ended the season in ninth place.

Arsenal's Welsh international full-back Walley Barnes follows the ball back to goalkeeper Jack Kelsey during the floodlit friendly match against Dinamo Moscow in Moscow in October 1954. A crowd of 90,000 Soviets saw one of the greatest clubs in the world go down 5-0 to the home team, such was the gulf between top British club sides and those in the rest of the world at that time. The European Cup was still some months away and even then it would be some years before British sides made a consistently good impression in European competition.

Arsenal's full-time playing staff pictured before the start of the 1955-6 season. Back row (left to right): Popple, Nicholas, Dove, Brasted, Smith, Wilkinson, Smailes, Cook, Vernon, Dooler. Middle: Wade, Guthrie, Walsh, Goring, Dodgin, Sullivan, Fotheringham, Kelsey, Holton, Herd, Oakes, Goy, Dickson. Front: Bowen, Evans, Tapscott, Clapton, Forbes, Barnes, Lawton, Flanagan, Bloomfield, Wills, Lishman. On ground: Goulden, Saxby, Haverty, Greenwood. The Gunners finished fifth in Division One and reached the last eight of the FA Cup.

In the 1956-7 FA Cup, Arsenal reached the quarter-finals, where they drew 2-2 at The Hawthorns. Huge crowds formed outsi thousands still outside. The attendance was 58,757.

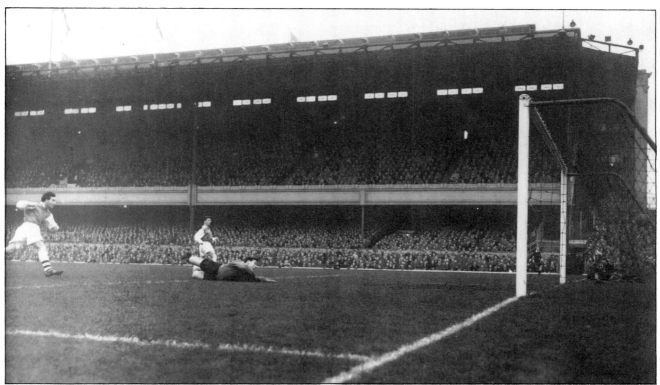

Vic Groves, a £30,000 signing from Leyton Orient, scores one of his two goals against Aston Villa at Highbury in November 1956. The despairing goalkeeper is Nigel Sims. Arsenal finished in fifth place, Villa went on to beat Manchester United in the FA Cup Final.

Highbury for the replay and these fans are queueing for stand tickets. When the box office closed after 45 minutes there were

Arsenal lost the 1957 quarter-final 2-1. Here, Albion goalkeeper Jim Sanders saves Danny Clapton's penalty to deny the Gunners.

Following a centre from Danny Clapton (left), Vic Groves opens the scoring against Luton at Highbury in the third game of the 1957-8 season. Ron Baynham is well beaten. Holton scored another and Arsenal won 2-0.

Inside-right Ray Swallow scores Arsenal's first goal in their 4-0 win against Aston Villa in October 1957. Swallow, a useful cricketer, was later transferred to Second Division Derby County and opened the batting for Derbyshire CCC.

Cliff Holton leaps to head the equaliser against Newcastle United at Highbury in November 1957. The Magpies' centre-half John Nesbitt has missed the ball whilst their skipper Jimmy Scoular appears to be making a 'back' for Holton. Arsenal still lost, though, 3-2.

A determined effort by Derek Tapscott beats Blackpool goalkeeper George Farm but the ball went wide and it was the Seasiders who eventually won this First Division game in January 1958, 3-2. Arsenal's great post-war era was now well and truly over and the Gunners ended the season in 12th place and were the subject of another FA Cup shock, this time knocked out of the third round by Third Division South club Northampton Town.

The last appearance in England of Manchester United's great pre-Munich side was at Highbury in February 1958, when a crowd of 63,578 were treated to a nine-goal thriller which saw the Gunners just squeezed out. Arsenal's first goal came from David Herd (centre of picture), who hammers the ball past Harry Gregg. The United defenders are Roger Byrne and Duncan Edwards.

Jack Kelsey, Stan Charlton (on ground), Jim Fotheringham and Gerry Ward (on one knee) are relieved to see the ball go narrowly past the Arsenal post. The United player is Bobby Charlton.

Stan Charlton (far left) fails to head clear a shot from Chelsea's Jimmy Greaves (on ground) at Highbury in March 1958. The Gunners won a nine-goal thriller by the odd goal with a hat-trick from David Herd.

Sixteen-year-old goalkeeper John Barton makes his League debut for Preston North End at Highbury in December 1958, gathering the ball here from Arsenal's John Barnwell. Barton helped his side to a 2-1 win but Arsenal ended the season in third place.

Two Everton defenders close in too late to prevent Vic Groves scoring at Highbury in January 1959. Groves scored twice in the Gunners' 3-1 win.

Arsenal reached the fifth round of the FA Cup in 1959 and drew 2-2 at Bramall Lane. This picture shows Kelsey stranded and Len Wills too far away as the Blades' outside-left Ron Simpson scores his side's first goal in the replay at Highbury. The Sheffield side won 3-0.

Blackburn's Derek Dougan stabs his side's first goal over the line at Highbury in March 1959. Jim Standen is the Gunners' 'keeper, Bill Dodgin the defender beaten to the ball by Dougan. The result was a 1-1 draw, Wills scoring Arsenal's goal from the penalty-spot.

Manchester City goalkeeper Bert Trautmann is grounded but right-back Ken Branagan clears off the line as David Herd rushes in at Highbury in September 1959. Arsenal won 3-1 but went on to finish only 13th in Division One.

Bolton's England goalkeeper Eddie Hopkinson dives at the feet of John Barnwell at Highbury in December 1960, when Arsenal won 5-1.

Former Arsenal forward Derek Tapscott laid on this goal for his teammate Brian Walsh at Highbury in Febuary 1961. Groves and McClelland look on in dismay. The Bluebirds won 3-2.

Vic Groves, now playing at wing-half, robs Leicester City's Albert Cheeseborough with Jack Kelsey also sliding in. Terry Neill is the other defender. Arsenal lost 3-1 in February 1961 and ended the season in 11th position.

Arsenal pictured before the start of the 1961-2 season, George Swindin's last as manager. The Gunners, still in a trough, ended the campaign in tenth place and went out of the FA Cup in the fourth round. Back row (left to right): Jim Magill, Mel Charles, Laurie Brown, Jack Kelsey, John McClelland, Alan Skirton, Allan Young, Terry Neill. Middle: George Swindin, Danny Clapton, Jim Snedden, Jackie Henderson, George Eastham, Vic Groves, Billy McCullough, Geoff Strong, Dave Bacuzzi, Bertie Mee (physiotherapist). Front: John McLeod, Gerry Ward, Len Wills, John Petts.

Mel Charles leaps over Burnley's Jimmy Adamson to head a brilliant second goal giving Adam Blacklaw no chance at Highbury on the opening day of the 1961-2 season. Charles scored both the Gunners' goals in a 2-2 draw against the team that was to finish First Division runners-up.

Blackpool goalkeeper Gordon West watches full-back Jimmy Armfield try to block a shot from Mel Charles (extreme right) at Highbury in October 1961, but the ball found its way into the net and Arsenal went on to win 3-0.

Blackburn's Fred Pickering and Arsenal's Laurie Brown in a heading duel at Highbury in March 1962.

Arsenal's new manager Billy Wright, the former Wolves and England half-back and holder of a record number of international caps, pictured on the day he took over in May 1962. With him is Mr Bob Wall, the famous secretary of the Arsenal club.

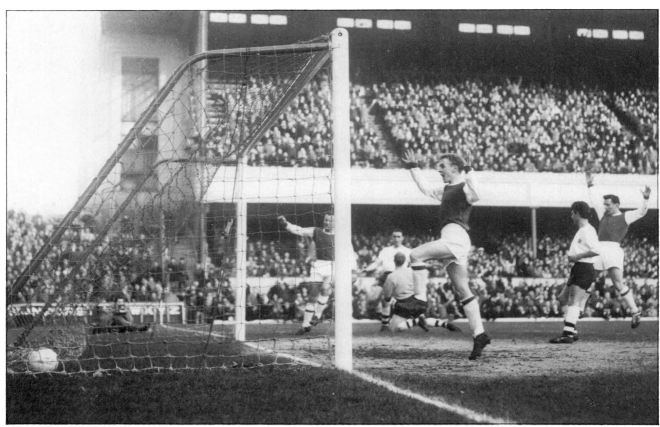

Arfon Griffiths leaps for joy as fellow Welshman Mel Charles (seen through the net) scores the Gunners' goal against Bolton at Highbury in January 1962. But Arsenal lost 2-1.

New boss and new star. Billy Wright shows centre-forward Joe Baker around Highbury in July 1962. Wright signed Baker, who was with Hibernian when he became the first player from a Scottish club to win an England cap, for an Arsenal record fee of £70,000 from AC Torino. Baker responded with 123 goals in 186 League and Cup games for the Gunners before a loss of form — and with it a place in Alf Ramsey's 1966 World Cup plans — led to his being transferred to Nottingham Forest for £65,000 in February that year.

Heads high at Highbury in August 1962 during the First Division game against Manchester United. Players (from left to right) are Moir and Herd of United and Magill of Arsenal. Arsenal lost 3-1. They ended the season in seventh place.

Arsenal first-teamers pictured before the start of the 1962-3 season. Back row (left to right): Jim Magill, Eddie Clamp, Vic Groves, Jack Kelsey, Billy McCullough, Jim Snedden, Laurie Brown, Terry Neill. Middle: Bertie Mee (physiotherpist), John Barnwell, Geoff Strong, George Eastham, Billy Wright (manager), John McLeod, John Petts, Alan Skirton, Joe Bacuzzi; Front: Joe Baker, Arfon Griffith, Gerry Ward.

Almost 20,000 spectators watched this friendly game between Arsenal and Spurs at White Hart Lane in January 1963, arranged after both clubs had suffered from a lack of football due to one of the worst winters in memory. John McClelland is beaten by Jimmy Greaves' first goal for Tottenham, who went on to win 3-1.

Billy Wright gets into an Arsenal strip and down to work with the players. Alas, although Wright had been an international star, he did not make a successful manager. Perhaps his 'nice guy' image did not fit happily with the emerging role of the modern manager.

Geoff Strong heads Arsenal's first goal at Craven Cottage in September 1963, despite the challenge of Alan Mullery and Bill Dodgin. Strong scored twice in the Gunners' 4-1 victory.

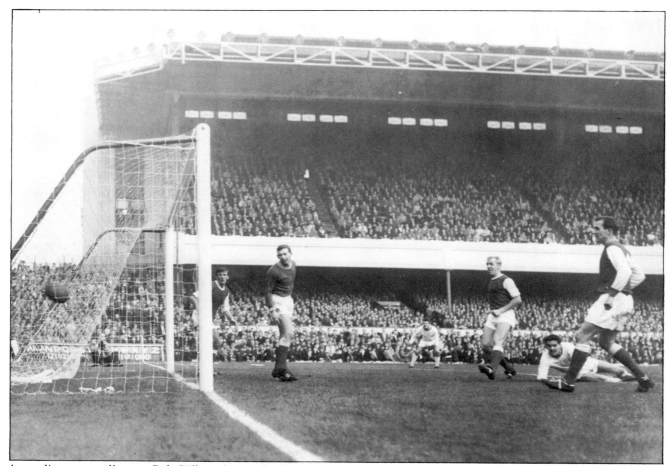

Arsenal's new goalkeeper Bob Wilson is caught flat-footed as Nottingham Forest's Frank Wignall (on ground) heads his side's second goal at Highbury in October 1963.

Billy Wright examines Highbury's new undersoil heating system watched by (left to right): Jim Magill, Ian Ure, John McLeod, Alan Skirton, George Eastham and Billy McCulloch. The system was installed in 1964 at a cost of some £10,000.

Chelsea's players look happy and no wonder. Centre-forward Barry Bridges has just scored their first goal against Arsenal at Stamford Bridge in November 1963. The Pensioners went on to win 3-1. Players (left to right) are: Barnwell, Wilson, McCulloch, Venables, Ure, Bridges and Murray.

George Eastham misses a penalty against Sheffield Wednesday at Highbury in March 1964 and the Gunners were held to a 1-1 draw. Poor Eastham had also failed from the spot the previous Saturday, when Arsenal were again held 1-1, this time by West Ham. These were dismal times for the Gunners, who finished eighth in Division One and lost to Liverpool in the fifth round of the FA Cup.

A spectator rushes on to the Highbury pitch after Leicester City are awarded a penalty during the First Division match in January 1965. The Gunners won 4-3.

Leicester's Gordon Banks dives at the ball as Arsenal's John Radford hurdles the great goalkeeper.

August 1966 and the Gunners' physioptherapist Bertie Mee is the new manager of Arsenal Football Club. He 'meets' th

players (from left to right): Terry Neill, John Radford, Tommy Baldwin, Frank McLintock, Bob Wilson and Don Howe.

Joe Baker gets high but Sheffield United goalkeeper Alan Hodgkinson gathers the ball at Highbury in November 1965. Baker, though, scored twice in a 6-2 win for Arsenal.

A great effort by John Radford (extreme right) against Manchester City at Highbury in January 1967 but the ball went just over the bar. Frank McLintock's goal gave Arsenal a 1-0 victory.

Arsenal goalkeeper Jim Furnell is beaten by a shot from inside-right Bobby Hope of West Brom for the Albion's first goal at Highbury in October 1966. The Throstles won 3-2.

Jim Furnell fails to stop George Best's goal in the 2-0 defeat by Manchester United at Highbury in February 1968.

Arsenal's Bobby Gould gets in a brilliantly executed header against Fulham at Craven Cottage in March 1968, but the effort was equally well saved by former Gunners' goalkeeper John McClelland, who signed for the Cottagers in December 1964. Arsenal won the game 3-1 on their way to finishing ninth in Division One.

It was North London derby time on the opening day of the 1968-9 season. Arsenal goalkeeper Bob Wilson bravely blocks a shot from Spurs' debutant 20-year-old Jimmy Pearce. Also pictured Arsenal defender Terry Neill. Arsenal won 2-1 with a goal from Radford and an own-goal from Beal.

Stoke goalkeeper John Farmer blocked this penalty from Terry Neill at Highbury in September 1968, but

the ball was scrambled into the net by Peter Simpson, although Neill is credited with the only goal of the game.

Bobby Gould raises his arms in delight as Frank McLintock rushes to congratulate him after he had scored Arsenal's first goal against Sheffield Wednesday at Highbury in January 1969. Radford scored Arsenal's second in a 2-0 win.

Burnley left-back Les Latcham looks as if he is about to handle this header from Arsenal left-winger Jimmy Robertson at Highbury in February 1969, but in fact he headed it off the line. The Clarets still went down 2-0, however.

Roger Smart of Third Division Swindon Town puts his side ahead in the 1969 Football League Cup Final against Arsenal at Wembley. It was one of the biggest Cup upsets for years.

The combined goal-line efforts of Gould, Storey and McNab cannot prevent Swindon's second goal, scored by Don Rogers (arm raised, centre of picture). Bob Wilson is already well out of it and Ian Ure can only look on in horror.

Bob Wilson and Peter Noble battle for the ball as Ian Ure and Bob McNab wait.

Radford leaps high but Ipswich Town's David Best punches the ball away at Highbury in October 1969. The result was a goalless draw.

George Armstrong takes avoiding action as Southampton goalkeeper Gerry Gurr block his shot. The sides drew 2-2 at Highbury in December 1969.

Sunderland's Jim Montgomery dives the wrong way for Peter Storey's penalty at Highbury in February 1970. Sunderland were beaten 3-1.

Peter Marinello, Arsenal's new £100,000 signing from Hibernian, skips a tackle from Chelsea's Eddie McCreadie at Highbury in January 1970, when the Gunners went down 3-0.

Crystal Palace's John Jackson blocks John Radford's effort in the Gunners' 2-0 win at Highbury in March 1970.

Frank McLintock stretches out a foot to intercept a pass from Keizer of Ajax during the Gunners' European Fairs Cup semi-final first leg 3-0 win at Highbury in April 1970. A 1-0 defeat in Holland in the second leg was a good enough result to send Arsenal into their first European Final.

John Radford rushes past the goalpost after heading Arsenal's second in the European Fairs Cup Final second-leg game at Highbury in April 1970. Charlie George (10) and George Armstrong also looked pretty pleased. Not so the Anderlecht goalkeeper Trappeniers.

This time Trappeniers punches clear from Eddie Kelly. Arsenal won 3-0 to give them a 4-3 aggregate win. Not only was it the Gunners' first European triumph, it was the first trophy of any note that the club had won for 17 years. A crowd of 51,612 saw the game.

Arsenal take a bus trip through North London with the Fairs Cup.

In their defence of the Fairs Cup, Arsenal reached the fourth round before being knocked out by 1.FC Köln. In this first-round first-leg game in Italy, John Radford heads one of his two goals against Lazio.

In the second-round second-leg tie at Highbury in November 1970, the Gunners completed the defeat of Sturm Graz of Austria. The Austrian goalkeeper makes a spectacular grab at the ball from Ray Kennedy.

Arsenal's first home game of the 1970-71 season saw them beat former European champions Manchester United

) with a hat-trick from John Radford. On this occasion, however, Radford's shot went wide of Stepney's post.

Jim Barron, the Nottingham Forest goalkeeper, punches over the bar from Arsenal's John Radford at Highbury in October 1970, when a hat-trick from Ray Kennedy and a goal from George Armstrong gave the Gunners a 4-0 victory on their way to an historic League and Cup double.

John Roberts seems to be making sure that Derby County's Dave Mackay does not win this heading duel at Highbury later the same month, when Arsenal won 2-0.

John Radford and Charlie George hug each other as Manchester City goalkeeper Joe Corrigan goes to pick the ball out of the net following Radford's goal at Highbury in February 1971. It proved to be the only goal of the game and set Arsenal further along the road to an historic success.

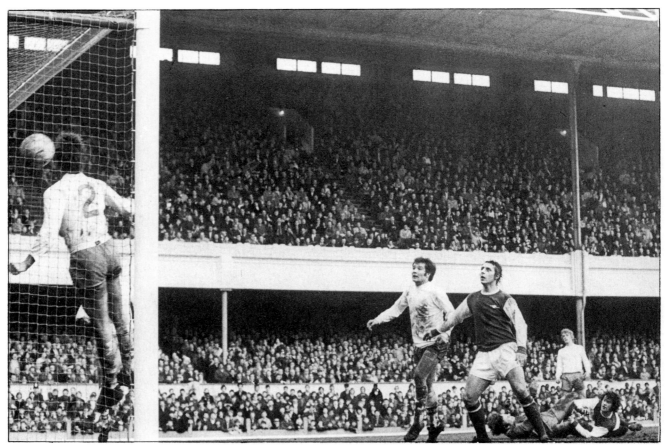

Blackpool right-back Terry Alcock makes a vain attempt to keep out Peter Storey's header at Highbury in March 1971 but it was the only goal of the game as the Gunners marched on to their first League Championship since 1953. The goalscorer is on the ground and John Radford is the Arsenal forward nearest the camera.

Arsenal substitute Eddie Kelly scores the winner against Stoke City in the penultimate match of the 1970-71 season as the Gunners inch nearer still to the title. Strangely, Arsenal had lost 5-0 at Stoke earlier in the season. A 1-0 win in their final match — at White Hart Lane of all places — clinched the Championship, one point ahead of Leeds United.

This mêlée in front of the Stoke goal resulted in a dramatic last-minute equaliser for the Gunners in the 1971 FA Cup semi-final at Hillsborough. Peter Storey scored from the spot — his second goal of the match — to earn Arsenal a replay, which they won 2-0 at Villa Park.

Peter Storey of Arsenal and Alec Lindsay of Liverpool tussle for the ball in the 1971 FA Cup Final.

Nine minutes from the end of extra-time in the 1971 FA Cup Final it seemed that the Gunners must go to a replay before knowing whether the coveted double would be theirs. Then Charlie George let fly from 20 yards to give Ray Clemence no chance and Arsenal had achieved their dream.

A happy Charlie George after scoring the goal which gave Arsenal the League and Cup double, only the second time it had been achieved this century.

Arsenal's League and Cup double winning squad pictured at Highbury in July 1971. Back row (left to right): Bob McNab, Ray Kennedy, Bob Wilson, John Roberts, Geoff Barnett, Peter Simpson, Peter Marinello. Front: Sammy Nelson, Peter Storey, John Radford, Pat Rice, Frank McLintock, Eddie Kelly, George Graham, George Armstrong. Missing: Charlie George and Jon Sammels.

Arsenal's Ray Kennedy heads towards goal during the Gunners' first-round second-leg European Cup game against Norwegian champions Strømgodset at Highbury In September 1971. Arsenal took the tie 7-1 on aggregate.

Peter Storey in action against Grasshoppers in November 1971. Arsenal won the first game in Switzerland 2-0 and then coasted into the third round of the European Cup with a 3-0 victory in this game at Highbury.

In the European Cup quarter-final, Arsenal were eliminated 3-1 on aggregate by Ajax Amsterdam. Here, the Dutch club's Blankenburg gets the ball away for a corner in the second leg at Highbury. After a 2-1 defeat in Holland, the Gunners lost 1-0 at home.

Hulsoff of Ajax heads clear from an Arsenal attack. The Gunners' number four is Peter Storey.

In defence of their League Championship title, Arsenal could manage only fifth place in 1971-2. In November they lost 2-1 at home to Manchester City. Here, George Armstrong has a shot blocked by Willie Donachie, who is about to collide with goalkeeper Joe Corrigan.

Eddie Kelly, watched by Pat Rice, beats Crystal Palace's John Jackson to put Arsenal in front at Highbury in November 1971. They went on to win 2-1.

In April, Arsenal beat Nottingham Forest 3-0 at Highbury. Ray Kennedy traps a high ball, challenged by Dave Serella.

Arsenal's reserve goalkeeper Geoff Barnett cannot stop this header from Allan Clarke (out of picture) for the only goal of the 1972 Centenary FA Cup Final. Barnett came in for the injured Bob Wilson — crocked in the semi-final — but could not be blamed for Arsenal's defeat at the hands of Leeds United.

September 1972 and Ray Kennedy tries a shot against Chelsea but the Stamford Bridge club's Peter Bonetti blocks his effort as David Webb looks on anxiously.

November 1972 and Coventry goalkeeper Bill Glazier punches the ball away from Peter Storey. Arsenal lost 2-0 and eventually ended the season as runners-up to Liverpool. They went out of the FA Cup in the semi-final, at the hands of Second Division Sunderland, who went on to score a shock Wembley victory over Leeds.

The same month and Charlie George takes to the air during the Gunners' 1-0 win against Everton at Highbury.

Tottenham's Jimmy Neighbour heads away from Pat Rice, watched by Arsenal's new signing Jeff Blockley at White Hart Lane in December 1972. Arsenal won 2-1 in front of 47,505 spectators.

After the glory of the double only three seasons earlier, the 1973-4 campaign was one of anticlimax for Arsenal, who ended it in tenth position and went out of both the FA Cup and the League Cup at an early stage. In September 1973, the Gunners beat Stoke City 2-1 at home. Here, Jeff Blockley finds himself the contents of a sandwich with three Stoke defenders.

Alan Ball causes all kinds of havoc in the Bradford City defence during the FA Cup fourth-round tie at Highbury in February 1973, which Arsenal won 2-0.

Brian Hornsby gets in a header against Coventry in December 1973 to score Arsenal's first goal in their 2-2 draw.

Little George Armstrong does his best in a heading duel with Liverpool's Chris Lawler at Highbury in November 1973. The Merseysiders won 2-0 and eventually finished runners-up to Leeds United.

January 1974 and Alan Ball opens the scoring against Norwich City. Ball scored both goals in Arsenal's 2-0 win. A week previously, the Gunners had knocked the Canaries out of the FA Cup.

Liam Brady (right) gets in his shot despite the attentions of Norwich's David Stringer.

After beating Norwich in the third round of the FA Cup, Arsenal met Aston Villa at Highbury and drew 1-1 before losing the replay at Villa Park. Bob Wilson looks cool enough as the ball goes narrowly wide of his post with Pat Rice looking a little more relieved.

Chelsea on the attack at Stamford Bridge in April 1974. Peter Houseman is grounded amongst Arsenal defenders Sammy Nelson, Peter Storey and Eddie Kelly. The Gunners won 3-1.

In October 1974, the Gunners drew 2-2 with QPR at Highbury with goals from Kidd and Radford, during the early part of a season which again saw their League fortunes founder. Don Givens of QPR forces his way through against Powling with Radford looking on.

West Ham's Billy Jennings gets in a forceful header, despite the attentions of Kelly and Mancini at Highbury in October 1974. Arsenal won this First Division match 3-0, but it was the Hammers who beat them in the FA Cup sixth round later that season.

Derby County's Peter Daniel tips the ball away from Brian Kidd at Highbury in November 1974. The Gunners beat them 3-1 but the Rams recovered to lift their second League Championship in four seasons.

Brian Kidd gets the better of this heading duel with John Craggs of newly-promoted Middlesbrough in November 1974. Kidd missed only two League games in 1974-5 and finished Arsenal's top scorer with 19 goals.

John Radford gets up high against Middlesbrough in Arsenal's 2-0 home win in November 1974. Brian Kidd is the Arsenal number 10.

Kevin Keegan is squeezed out by Peter Simpson and Terry Mancini at Highbury in February 1975. Alan Ball's two goals, one from the penalty-spot, saw Arsenal take both points.

Leicester goalkeeper Mark Wallington takes Arsenal's Brian Kidd with him as he dives for the ball during the FA Cup fifth-round tie at Highbury in February 1975. The result was a goalless draw and after the sides also drew at Filbert Street, Arsenal eventually went through with an extra-time goal in the second replay, also at Leicester.

Brian Kidd connects to this cross which was missed by Kevin Lock of West Ham in the FA Cup quarter-final game at Highbury in March 1975. The Hammers won 2-0 and Arsenal's season became simply an academic exercise from that moment.

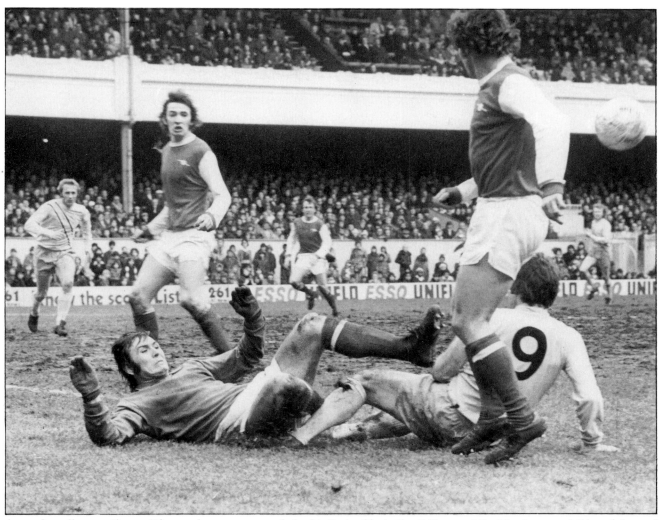

Arsenal goalkeeper Jimmy Rimmer becomes entangled with Stoke City's Geoff Hurst whilst Matthews and Rice of Arsenal wonder what they can do to help. The teams drew 1-1 in March 1975.

Arsenal's first-team squad at the beginning of the dismal 1975-6 season which saw the Gunners finish 17th in the League, crash out of the FA Cup 3-0 at Wolves, and also make an early exit from the League Cup. Back row (left to right): Bobby Campbell (coach), Brian Hornsby, Terry Mancini, John Matthews, Jimmy Rimmer, Brian Kidd, Geoff Barnett, Trevor Ross, Richard Powling, Wilf Rostron, Fred Street (physiotherapist); Front: Pat Rice, Alex Cropley, Sammy Nelson, Eddie Kelly, John Radford, Bertie Mee (manager), Alan Ball, Peter Storey, Peter Simpson, George Armstrong, Liam Brady.

Jimmy Rimmer pulls down a dangerous cross as Stoke City's Denis Smith (5), gets high above the Gunners' defence at Highbury in Arsenal's first home game of the 1975-6 campaign. Stoke won 1-0.

Alan Ball disappears beneath Leicester City's substitute Bobby Lee during the 1-1 draw at Highbury in September 1975. David O'Leary tries to intercept. A crowd of barely 22,000 watched the game, a far cry from the days when Highbury was packed to the rafters week after week.

Jimmy Rimmer and Peter Simpson are left flat-footed as Asa Hartford opens the scoring for Manchester City at Highbury in October 1975. City won 3-2, which meant that Arsenal had won only two of their opening ten games.

Manchester United's Stewart Houston gets the better of Liam Brady at Highbury in November 1975. The Gunners won 3-1 and the more attractive opposition saw an attendance of just over 40,000.

Ipswich substitute Keith Bertschin scores with his first touch of the ball to level the scores at Highbury in April 1976. Arsenal had taken the lead through Frank Stapleton's header (below) but the Suffolk club fought back to take both points.

In March 1976, Arsenal manager Bertie Mee announced that he would retire at the end of the season. Mee had taken over from Billy Wright in 1966, on a 'temporary' basis, and led the Gunners to the League and Cup double five years later. Now the team was struggling and after two particularly difficult seasons, Mee was feeling the pressure. It was understandable that he felt it was time for a younger man to try to revitalise the flagging fortunes of one of the greatest football clubs in the world.

In July 1976, former Arsenal defender Terry Neill took over as manager at Highbury. Neill made 241 League appearances for the Gunners before becoming one of the youngest manager's in the League when he was appointed to Hull City in November 1970. Neill, also a former chairman of the PFA, and skipper and manager of Northern Ireland — he won 59 caps — had succeeded Bill Nicholson at Spurs in September 1974. Now he made the short trip across North London to return to his first senior club. Initially, Neill found it difficult to be in charge of former playing colleagues, but in seven years in the job he would guide Arsenal to three successive FA Cup Finals and a European Final.

On the opening day of the 1976-7 season, newly-promoted Bristol City scored a shock 1-0 victory at Highbury. Pat Rice (2), Alan Ball and David O'Leary can only watch as City's Paul Cheesley heads the only goal of the game. It was hardly the start that a new manager wanted but by the end of the season the Gunners were in eighth position, an improvement of nine places on the previous campaign.

Powling and Stapleton of Arsenal and Everton's Ken McNaught are involved in an aerial ballet during the game at Highbury in September 1976. Arsenal won 3-1 with goals from Brady, Stapleton and Macdonald.

Neill's first signing for Arsenal was that of the Newcastle United centre-forward Malcolm Macdonald, for whom Arsenal paid out £333,333. Macdonald never won any of the game's top club honours — he played in losing Cup Finals for Newcastle and Arsenal — but he was capped for England and with Arsenal formed a useful scoring partnership with Frank Stapleton.

A pat on the head for Malcolm Macdonald from Queen's Park Rangers' goalkeeper Phil Parkes in the First Division London derby game in October 1976. Arsenal won by the odd goal in five.

The following week, Macdonald looked less happy. He had just collided with Stoke's Peter Shilton, who comforts his opponent until qualified help arrives. The Gunners won 2-0, but were about to embark on a run of three consecutive defeats in which they conceded 11 goals.

Malcolm Macdonald outjumps Newcastle's Aidan McCaffery to score Arsenal's second goal against his old club at Highbury in December 1976. Macdonald scored a hat-trick as Arsenal won 5-3.

QPR's Dave Needham gets in a tackle on Malcolm Macdonald at Highbury in October 1977, but Macdonald had the last laugh. He went on to score the only goal of the game. Arsenal's fortunes were improving under Terry Neill. They climbed still further up the table to finish in fifth place and reached the FA Cup Final and the League Cup semi-final.

At Highbury in November 1977, Ian Wallace of Coventry City, flanked by David Price and David O'Leary, tries a shot at goal but the ball went wide. The sides drew 1-1, Arsenal's goal coming from a Mick Coop own-goal.

David O'Leary hammers home Arsenal's third goal against Chelsea on Boxing Day 1977. Peter Bonetti, the Chelsea goalkeeper, looks up helplessly. A holiday crowd of over 46,000 saw the game at Highbury.

Malcolm Macdonald wheels away after scoring one of his two goals against Manchester United at Highbury in April 1978. Brady scored the Gunners' other goal in this 3-1 victory.

Malcolm Macdonald (in the background, arms raised) watches as his shot is deflected over the line by an Orient defender for Arsenal's second goal at Stamford Bridge in April 1978. Arsenal beat their Third Division London rivals 3-0 to set up a Wembley meeting with Ipswich Town. With Ipswich meeting West Brom at Highbury, it was the first time for many years that both FA Cup semi-finals had been staged in London.

Graham Rix finishes off a solo run to score Arsenal's third g

the semi-final against Orient. The goalkeeper is John Jackson.

Frank Stapleton tries a shot at goal during the 1978 FA Cup Final against Ipswich Town at Wembley. Kevin Beattie is too late with his challenge and George Burley is too far away to get in a tackle. But the game was wrapped up by Ipswich's Roger Osborne, who scored the only goal and was then so overcome with emotion and exhaustion that he was substituted. For Arsenal it had been a disappointing end to a highly encouraging season.

Roger Osborne hammers home the winner of the 1978 FA Cup Final. Willie Young is caught of balance. Full-back Pat Rice is on the goal-line but cannot prevent the goal.

In November 1978, Arsenal gained some revenge for their FA Cup Final defeat by hammering Ipswich 4-1 in a First Division game at Highbury. Frank Stapleton scored a hat-trick and here he nets his second past Paul Cooper. Arsenal finished the season one place below Ipswich in seventh place.

David Price (centre) scores Arsenal's goal in the 1-1 draw against Southampton in the FA Cup quarter-final game at The Dell in March 1979. The Gunners won the replay 2-0 and then saw off Wolves in the semi-final. Yet they took a long time to make it past the third round, where it needed five games to dispose of Sheffield Wednesday.

Alan Sunderland scores the Gunners' second goal against Wolves at Villa Park in the 1979 FA Cup semi-final. Earlier, Frank Stapleton had given Arsenal the lead.

Brian Talbot and Alan Sunderland arrived together for this cross from David Price, but it was Talbot who was adjudged to have got the decisive touch to put Arsenal ahead after only 12 minutes of the 1979 FA Cup Final. There were still some hurdles to cross before Arsenal lifted the Cup, however. It was only in the last five minutes that the game really came to life. Two minutes before half-time, Stapleton appeared to have put the result beyond doubt but with four minutes of the match remaining, McQueen pulled back a goal and then McIlroy equalised. United were buoyant after fighting back from a seemingly hopeless position but with only seconds left on the clock, Sunderland stabbed home the winner.

Brian Talbot (nearest camera) and Alan Sunderland celebrate Arsenal's first goal in the prone position and below Frank Stapleton heads a late goal against Manchester United in the 1979 FA Cup Final. Sunderland netted the winner in the last minute as extra-time loomed.

Happy Arsenal at Wembley in 1979.

Pat Rice, the Arsenal captain, holds up the FA Cup after the presentation by HRH The Prince of Wales.

Alan Sunderland beats two Magdeburg defenders but mistimed his header in this European Cup-winners' Cup tie at Highbury in October 1979. He later scored to help Arsenal to a 2-1 win to take to East Germany for the second leg.

This time Sunderland is bang on target and receives the congratulations of his teammates after scoring the second goal in Arsenal's 3-1 win over Coventry at Highbury in December 1979, on their way to finishing fourth in Division One.

Sunderland (hidden behind Stapleton, second left) also scored twice in this FA Cup third-round replay at Highbury against Cardiff City in January 1980.

Willie Young (number 6) hits the rebound to score Arsenal's fifth goal against IFK Gothenburg in the Cup-winners' Cup third-round first-leg match at Highbury in March 1980.

Paul Vaessen (obscured by Alan Sunderland) has just scored the only goal of the Cup-winners' Cup semi-final second-leg game in Turin in April 1980. It gave Arsenal a 2-1 aggregate win, but in the Final they lost 5-4 on penalties to Valencia in Brussels.

West Ham's Trevor Brooking scores the only goal of the 1980 FA Cup Final, the Gunners' third appearance in a Wembley Cup Final in as many years.

Paul Mariner of Ipswich Town takes on two Arsenal players, Steve Walford and Frank Stapleton, in the 1-1 draw at Highbury at Christmas 1980.

Coventry's Brian Roberts tries to stop Brian Talbot during the 2-2 draw at Highbury in January 1981. Earlier in the month, Arsenal's interest in the FA Cup was ended at the first hurdle by Everton and they had already gone out of the League Cup. In the First Division, though, the Gunners did well and finished in third place.

Coventry's Mark Hateley (centre) and Brian Roberts (right) are powerless to prevent John Hollins shooting for goal in the Highbury draw.

Manchester City's Asa Hartford (left) attempts to block a shot from Arsenal's Chris Whyte as Tommy Caton (later to join Arsenal) looks on. The Gunners beat City 1-0 at Highbury in October 1981 but it was Meade who scored the vital goal.

Alan Sunderland tries a shot but the ball has eluded him. Everton's defence is in disarray with goalkeeper Jim Arnold helpless on the floor. McDermott scored the only goal of the game and Arsenal picked up both points.

Alan Sunderland (second left) scores Arsenal's second goal against West Ham at Highbury in the 2-0 win in May 1982. The Gunners won four out of their last five League games to end the season in fifth place.

It was a surprise when Tottenham Hotspur allowed long-serving goalkeeper Pat Jennings to join rivals Arsenal for only £45,000 in August 1977. At 32 years of age, they obviously thought his best days were behind him. Yet Jennings went on to make 380 senior appearances for the Gunners, appeared in three FA Cup Finals and extended his already impressive international career to a then British record of 119 caps. In May 1985, Jennings enjoyed a testimonial game against Spurs at Highbury, when 23,252 spectators paid tribute to him. This picture shows Jennings in action during the game. Although he had announced his retirement, he came back to help Spurs the following season and was fit enough to play for Northern Ireland in the 1986 World Cup Finals. Altogether Jennings totted up 757 League appearances for Watford (his first club), Spurs and Arsenal.

John Hawley (left) scores Arsenal's third goal in their 4-1 victory over Southampton at Highbury in the last game of the 1981-2 season. The Saints player is Chris Nichol. The attendance was 28,534.

Lee Chapman attacks with Gordon McQueen of Manchester United in pursuit during the 1983 FA Cup semi-final at Villa Park. Tony Woodcock scored the Gunners' goal in a 2-1 defeat. Arsenal also lost to United in both legs of the League Cup semi-final.

Tony Woodcock in action against Southampton in April 1983, a season in which Arsenal finished tenth in Division One. Woodcock, a former Forest and 1.FC Cologne player, scored five goals for Arsenal at Villa Park in October 1983.

Stewart Robson is carried off by manager Terry Neill. Robson joined the Gunners as an apprentice and made 151 League appearances before being transferred to West Ham for £700,000 in January 1987 and moved to Coventry in 1990-91.

David O'Leary joined Arsenal as an apprentice in June 1973 to begin an illustrious career. Capped 64 times by the Republic of Ireland, O'Leary had made over 500 League appearances for Arsenal by the end of the 1991-2 season.

Terry Neill (left) vacated the Arsenal manager's seat in December 1983, under mounting pressure to provide the Gunners w[...] another major success. He was replaced by Don Howe (right), the club's former England full-back, who was appointed caretak[...]

ss on Neill's departure and confirmed as manager the following April. In his first season, Howe guided Arsenal to sixth place
t was unable to bring trophies to Highbury and in March 1986 asked to be released from his contract.

Charlie Nicholas, Arsenal's flamboyant striker, gets a telling-off from the referee. The former Celtic man cost the Gunners £650,000 when he signed in June 1983. He scored 34 goals in 151 League games before moving to Aberdeen for £400,000 in January 1988.

Nicholas gets past Luton Town's Mal Donaghy on the opening day of the 1983-4 season. Arsenal won 2-1.

Steve Williams on the ball against West Ham in March 1985. Mariner and Robson scored in a 2-1 win for the Gunners, who were on their way to finishing seventh in the First Division.

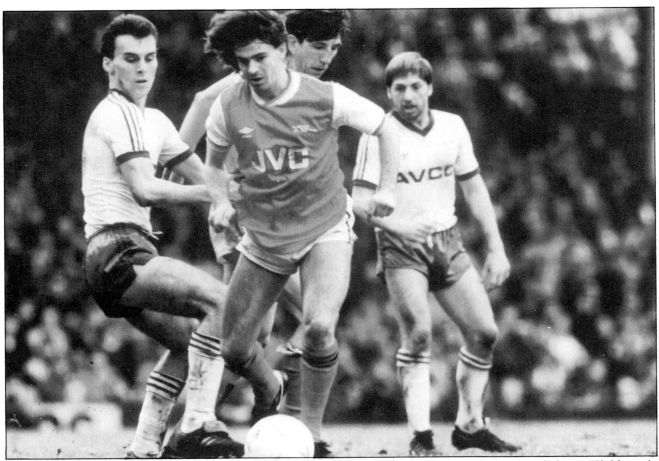

Charlie Nicholas runs through the Hammers' defence. A crowd of only 25,818 saw this London derby at Highbury in March 1985, underlining the trough through which Arsenal were travelling at the time.

John Lukic fails to stop this penalty against Stoke City at the Victoria Ground in March 1930 as Arsenal went down 2-0. Only 7,371 watched the Potters' third win of the season as they went on to finish 23 points adrift at the bottom of Division One.

Paul Mariner (right) is trying to worry Stoke City's Alan Hudson at the Victoria Ground in March 1985. Hudson joined Arsenal from Stoke in December 1976 for £200,000 and went back there via a spell in the NASL and with Chelsea.

Tony Adams lunges into a tackle against Neil Webb at the City Ground in September 1986, when Forest won 1-0.

David Rocastle (right) and Forest's Garry Birtles both take a tumble. Arsenal ended the 1986-7 season in fourth place under new manager George Graham, their former player.

Niall Quinn of Arsenal in action at Hillborough in February 1987. The tall striker scored Arsenal's goal in the 1-1 draw against Sheffield Wednesday.

Charlie Nicholas (second left) scores one of his two goals in the 1987 League Cup Final win over Liverpool. In the semi-final, the Gunners took three games to dispose of North London rivals, Tottenham.

Nicholas wheels away in celebration as Liverpool's Gary Gillespie appeals in vain for an infringement against the Arsenal man.

Nicholas (number 10) strikes again, beating the despairing lunge of Liverpool's Bruce Grobbelaar. The Gunners won 2-1 to lift the League Cup for the first time, although they had reached two previous Finals in the 1960s. This was expected to be the launch pad for Nicholas to move to greater things but he was sold to Aberdeen after playing in only three matches the following season.

The now traditional post-Wembley victory team group. This time it is Arsenal's turn after their 1987 League Cup Final win.

John Lukic, Paul Davis and skipper Tony Adams acknowledge their fans after the Wembley defeat of Liverpool.

David Rocastle, Paul Davis and Michael Thomas with the League Cup, now sponsored by Littlewoods. Rocastle later went to Leeds for £2 million and Thomas to Liverpool for £1.5 million.

Strikers Alan Smith and Charlie Nicholas hold the Littlewoods Cup. The two front men played only three times together, Smith went on to win England caps and head the League scoring lists in 1989-90 and 1990-91 — but Nicholas would return to Scotland to seek success.

Alan Smith and Nottingham Forest's Lee Glover battling for a high ball at the City Ground in September 1987. It was Smith who scored the only goal of the game. Arsenal finished the season sixth in Division One and were knocked out of the FA Cup quarter-finals by Forest, but they went all the way to Wembley again in the League Cup.

Substitute Martin Hayes (14) scores for Arsenal in the 1988 Littlewoods Cup Final against Luton Town. Luton's reserve goalkeeper Andy Dibble, on for the injured Les Sealey, saved Nigel Winterburn's penalty to prevent Arsenal opening up a two-goal lead and Brian Stein scored twice, including a last-minute winner, to give the Hatters a 3-2 victory.

Alan Smith (out of picture) scores Arsenal's second goal of the 1988 Littlewoods Cup Final.

In October 1988, Arsenal won the Mercantile Credit Centenary Trophy at Villa Park, beating Manchester United 2-1 after earlier wins over QPR and Liverpool. Here, the victorious Arsenal team show off the trophy which celebrated 100 years of the Football League.

Lee Dixon and Paul Merson with the Mercantile Credit Trophy. A crowd of 22,182 saw the Final.

Michael Thomas and Paul Davis scored the Gunners' goals in the Villa Park win over Manchester United.

Arsenal's Brian Marwood (right) and Spurs' Icelandic international Gudni Bergsson in action. The Gunners beat their old rivals twice in 1988-9 on the way to the League Championship, Arsenal's first Division One title since the double season of 1970-71.

Arsenal met Liverpool five times in 1988-9, losing a Littlewoods Cup tie after a second replay and meeting the Merseysiders twice in the League with epic consequences. Here, Alan Smith (right) and Steve Nicol chase a through ball. Smith scored in both League games against the Anfield club.

Steve Bould is grounded and can only watch as John Barnes and Lee Dixon battle it out.

Paul Merson cuts between Norwich City's Mark Bowen and Andy Linighan, who later joined the Highbury club for £1.2 million in July 1990. The sides drew 0-0 at Carrow Road in December 1988 but Arsenal won 5-0 at home in May.

Norwich's Dale Gordon tries to scoop the ball from the path of Kevin Richardson, a £200,000 signing from Watford.

Michael Thomas (second right) scores Arsenal's first goal in the 2-1 win over Manchester United in December 1988. Merson hit Arsenal's second. Later in the season Arsenal gained a valuable point at Old Trafford.

Paul Merson outpaces Chris Fairclough in the 2-0 win over Tottenham Hotspur at Highbury in January 1989. Merson ended the season as Arsenal's second-highest League scorer with ten goals, well behind Alan Smith's 23.

*Opposite page:* Steve Bould and Gary Pallister of Middlesbrough in the Gunners' 1-0 win at Ayresome Park in May 1989.

*Left:* Alan Smith in action in the same match, again Pallister is the challenger. Smith joined the Gunners from Leicester City for £750,000 in March 1987. Following that transfer he was loaned back to Leicester for the rest of the season but then became a vital member of the Arsenal line-up.

*Below:* Alan Smith (second left) scores Arsenal's first goal in the 52nd minute of the crucial last game of the 1988-9 season, against Liverpool at Anfield. But the Gunners, who had let a 19-point lead slip from their grasp, needed to win by a two-goal margin to claim the title.

In the dying seconds at Anfield, Michael Thomas (centre) scores the goal that won the 1988-9 Football League Championship. It is doubtful whether the title has ever been gained in more dramatic fashion.

A moment of quiet reflection for John Lukic and Tony Adams. In May 1990, Lukic returned to Leeds for £1 million.

The goalscorers at Anfield — Michael Thomas and Alan Smith with the League trophy.

Arsenal maintained their 'old boy' policy when they appointed former player George Graham as manager in May 1986. In his first season back at Highbury he steered the club to fourth place in Division One and to victory in the Littlewoods Cup. The following year Arsenal lost the Littlewoods Final to Luton, but in 1988-9 Graham became the fifth Arsenal manager to take the club to the League Championship.

Tony Adams and his team with the League Championship trophy after the defeat of Liverpool.

More celebrations as the Gunners players bask in the limelight after their nail-biting victory.

Another success for Arsenal. In July 1989, they won the Makita International Tournament at Wembley, beating FC Porto and then Liverpool, both 1-0. Here are the victorious Gunners with the trophy.

Steve Bould, who scored the only goal of the match, with the Makita International Tournament trophy after the win over Liverpool.

Arsenal opened the 1989-90 season with a 4-1 defeat at Old Trafford. *Above:* Gus Caesar gets in a tackle as Nigel Winterburn (left) watches. *Below:* Lee Dixon clears the ball. Arsenal ended the season in fourth place and were eliminated early on from both the FA Cup and Littlewoods Cup.

Swedish international midfielder Anders Limpár (left) arrived from Cremonese for £1 million in July 1990. Alan Smith (right) scored 27 League and Cup goals to end the 1990-91 season as Arsenal's leading scorer for the fourth season in succession.

The unacceptable face of football. In October 1990, Arsenal and Manchester United players were involved in an unseemly brawl at Old Trafford. Part of Arsenal's punishment for their part in the affair was the loss of two points, yet at the end of the season the Gunners had overcome that handicap to lift the League Championship again.

Towards the end of 1990-91, Arsenal nurtured dreams of another League and Cup double. Alas, that dream ended when the Gunners were beaten 3-1 by Tottenham Hotspur in the first FA Cup semi-final staged at Wembley. The defeat began with this brilliant goal from a free-kick by Paul Gascoigne after Limpár had fouled Lineker with only five minutes played.

Five minutes later, Gary Lineker scored the first of his two goals against Arsenal in the 1991 FA Cup semi-final, poking the ball over the line.

Alan Smith made it 2-1 just before half-time, beating Mabbutt in the air before heading the ball past Erik Thorstvedt.

Arsenal had already regained the League Championship trophy when they met Coventry City in the last match of the 1990-91 season and hammered them 6-1 with Limpár scoring a hat-trick. Here, the Gunners celebrate with the Barclays League trophy.

Two for the price of one. Arsenal, the 1990-91 League Champions, pictured with the Barclays trophy and the original League Championship trophy, first competed for in the days long before sponsorship.

Anders Limpár and Nigel Winterburn with the Football League Championship trophy.

This time it is the turn of David Seaman and Steve Bould to parade the trophy.

Lee Dixon gets to a high ball with Sampdoria's Orlando in close attendance. The Gunners lost this Makita game at Wembley 3-2 on penalties in August 1991, having earlier beaten Panathinaikos at Highbury.

In September 1991, Arsenal drew 2-2 at Elland Road but at the end of the season Leeds United had captured the Gunners' League title. Here, Gary Speed gets in a tackle on David O'Leary. O'Leary was in his 17th season with the Highbury club.

Back in Europe, Arsenal met FK Austria Memphis in the first round of the 1991-2 European Cup. Alan Smith has just scored one of his four goals in the first-leg game at Highbury which the Gunners won 6-1.

Paul Merson (right) chases a through ball in Vienna, Arsenal went down 1-0 but it hardly mattered with such an enormous lead from the first game.

In the second round of the 1991-2 European Cup, Arsenal went out 4-2 on aggregate to Benfica, drawing 1-1 in Portugal before an 80,000 crowd in the first leg. Merson is in action again.

Nigel Winterburn gets in a tackle on Benfica's Yuran at Highbury, where Arsenal lost 3-1 after extra-time. Talk now concerned the apparent gulf between English and European soccer as a result of the ban on Football League clubs after the Heysel tragedy.

Paul Merson is bypassed by Leeds United's Gary McAllister as David Batty watches. United were on the verge of stealing Arsenal's crown.

Ian Wright (left) was the Football League's leading scorer with 29 goals in 1991-2. Leeds United's Chris Whyte (right) was originally given a free transfer by the Gunners.

Nigel Winterburn gets his shot despite the attention of Leeds United's Rodney Wallace.

David Hillier congratulates Paul Merson who scored three goals in the 4-1 win over Crystal Palace at Highbury in April 1992.

This time it is Merson's turn to congratulate Campbell who also scored in the rout of Palace.

Kevin Campbell, who joined Arsenal as a schoolboy, was second-highest scorer in 1991-2.

Ian Wright, whose striking rate was still not enough to impress England boss Graham Taylor.

Paul Merson, whose 12 goals gave him joint third place with Alan Smith in the Gunners' list in 1991-2.

Colin Pates, a £500,000 signing from Charlton who went on loan to Brighton in 1991-2.

Perry Groves, signed from Colchester United for £50,000 in 1986, left for Southampton in August 1992 for £750,000.

David Hillier, came to Highbury as a schoolboy in 1985 and made 27 appearances in 1991-2, scoring one goal.

Norwegian international defender Pål Lydersen, joined Arsenal from IK Start for £500,000 in November 1991.

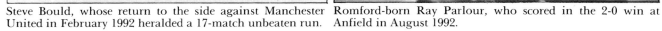

Steve Bould, whose return to the side against Manchester United in February 1992 heralded a 17-match unbeaten run.

Romford-born Ray Parlour, who scored in the 2-0 win at Anfield in August 1992.

David Seaman (left) joined Arsenal from QPR in May 1990 for £1.3 million, a British record for a goalkeeper. Andy Linighan (above), a £1.2 million signing from Norwich City in July 1990.